What is
Migration History?

What is History?

John H. Arnold, *What is Medieval History?*

Peter Burke, *What is Cultural History?* 2nd edition

John C. Burnham, *What is Medical History?*

Pamela Kyle Crossley, *What is Global History?*

Christiane Harzig and Dirk Hoerder, with Donna Gabaccia, *What is Migration History?*

J. Donald Hughes, *What is Environmental History?*

Stephen Morillo, with Michael F. Pavkovic, *What is Military History?*

What is Migration History?

CHRISTIANE HARZIG
AND DIRK HOERDER

with Donna Gabaccia

polity

First published in 2009 by Polity Press

Polity Press
65 Bridge Street
Cambridge CB2 1UR, UK

Polity Press
350 Main Street
Malden, MA 02148, USA

ISBN-13: 978-0-7456-4335-9
ISBN-13: 978-0-7456-4336-6 (pb)

A catalogue record for this book is available from the British Library.

Typeset in 10.5 on 12 pt Sabon
by SNP Best-set Typesetter Ltd., Hong Kong

The publisher has used its best endeavours to ensure that the URLs for
external websites referred to in this book are correct and active at the
time of going to press. However, the publisher has no responsibility for
the websites and can make no guarantee that a site will remain live or
that the content is or will remain appropriate.

Every effort has been made to trace all copyright holders, but if any have
been inadvertently overlooked the publisher will be pleased to include
any necessary credits in any subsequent reprint or edition.

For further information on Polity, visit our website:
www.politybooks.com

Dedicated to Christiane Harzig
who loved to teach migration and women's history
and whose life was cut short by cancer before this book was
finished
      by her husband Dirk Hoerder
      and by Donna Gabaccia, her friend since 1979,
      who completed the parts she could no longer write.

Contents

Detailed Contents

Maps

Preface

This introduction to the field of migration history provides a synthesis of past and present research approaches, emphasizing its interdisciplinary and worldwide character. We begin with scholarly images of emigration/immigration popular from the 1970s to the present (chapter 1) and point to questions they fail to address. We next provide a survey of migrations through human history (chapter 2). In chapter 3, we outline the classic theories of migration and cultural interaction that developed, mostly in the Atlantic World, after the 1880s and turn to important interpretative innovations emerging in Latin American and Caribbean societies and in Japan in the 1930s. While recognizing that migrations may be complex and involve several stages and stopovers, we propose a systems approach which comprehensively deals with three phases of migration processes: the culture of origin and departure, the actual move, and the process of insertion/acculturation into the receiving society (chapter 4). We then turn to major contemporary issues of research, such as race and gender, access to citizenship, transnational and transcultural lives, human agency and victimization, family economies, and migrant entrepreneurship (chapter 5). In conclusion, we discuss the future development of migration (chapter 6). Throughout we provide sparse annotation but include suggestions for further reading, selected generally from recent work. In chapter 3 we also annotate in more detail studies characteristic of the development of the field. Throughout the text we treat migration as a global phenomenon and introduce appropriate historical and historiographical examples, in order to explicate particular issues and regions as well as to illustrate migrant men's and women's lives. As we write, it seems that migration history is transforming into interdisciplinary migration studies, which draws on the social sciences and humanities and focuses broadly on transcultural societal studies.

C. H., D. H., D. G.

1
Introduction: Popular Views – Scholarly Reconceptualizations

In the century and a half of national perspectives in historiography from the 1830s to the 1960s, emigration as departure from the nation was little studied and immigration received attention in terms of "assimilation" to the institutions and culture of the receiving society. By the 1970s, scholars recognized many of the approaches to migrations worldwide to be limited and skewed.

- The modernization paradigm posited that high levels of mobility began with industrialization and urbanization.
- Historians divided people's moves into emigration and immigration, though each emigrant–immigrant was one and the same person.
- Scholars considered European migrants' voyages across the Atlantic Ocean as the model for all migration and viewed Atlantic crossings as westbound only. So did popular discourse on mobility in the United States, recommending "Go West, young man!"
- Women were hardly mentioned – all migrants seemed to be men. Gender was not a category.
- Race was not a category either – all migrants seemed to be whites.
- Scholars sharply segregated slavery, the forced and involuntary migrations of African men and women, from "free" human mobility, as in "the peopling of the Americas."

- From China, only "coolies" were said to have moved to plantations. Those going to North America all ended up in Chinatowns – if the literature is to be believed.
- Migration researchers considered many societies of the world as basically sedentary and thus of no interest.

In such views, the world's only migrant-receiving region was a vague, generic "America" – not the Americas or particular societies in the Americas. Similarly, migrants left from undifferentiated continents – Europe, China, and Africa – rather than from specific societies of origin. This limited perspective elevated the United States to the paradigmatic country of immigration. The continents sent forth differently endowed people: those who made free decisions, those who could be enslaved, and those who were mere coolies.

Even these opinions raised many questions, however: Did all immigrants like "America" or did some of them return? Was "America" the United States or did men and women also go to Canada, Brazil, Argentina, or Mexico? How did Europe's cities grow if only men emigrated? What did young women from Europe's many cultural regions do? If, in Russia, serfdom tied peasants to the soil, how did the factories of Moscow and St Petersburg get their labour forces, and how was Siberia settled? Did people in the many cultures of India never move? Were Africa's many societies not linked through migrations? If people were sedentary, who created the tenth-century interfaith Mediterranean World that encompassed North Africa, the Eastern Mediterranean (West Asia), and Europe's southern littoral?

One example illustrates the complexity of migration hidden behind these questions. Popular imagination created a generic nineteenth-century "John Chinaman." In fact, migrants came from only two southern provinces of the huge empire. They spoke different dialects. They migrated voluntarily as well as under indenture. Since the mid-fifteenth century, their ancestors had formed a disapora in Southeast Asia. In the late twentieth century, migrants came from "three Chinas" – the People's Republic, Taiwan, and Hong Kong – and from diasporic settlements across the globe. Men and women of Chinese culture arriving in Canada between 1980 and 2000 hailed from 132 different countries of prior settlement and spoke some one hundred different languages and dialects. As this example suggests, migrations are complex, often global phenomena; migrants depart from specific places and select their destinations from among many cultures.

The traditional *emigration–immigration dichotomy* does not reflect such complexity. Rather, it suggests a mono-directional one-way move from a "home" in one state to a foreign "new world" – where, myths have assumed, everything would be better. It describes migrants moving either from a nation to an ethnic enclave or from a limited old world to unlimited new opportunities. The term *migration*, by contrast, implies multiple options: mobility may be many-directional and multiple, temporary or long-term, voluntary or forced. Within a range of options, migrant men and women make decisions. Rather than deal with "flows" of people or "waves" of migration, migration history studies the agency of men and women who, within their capabilities, negotiate societal options and constraints in pursuit of life-plans. Migration history looks at both ends of mobility: What does it mean for families, urban neighbourhoods and villages, or whole societies to lose members? What does it mean for societies of destination to receive "human capital"?

The societies between which men and women move have been contrasted as "home" – a term which conveys feelings of belonging and protection – and "foreign," which conveys alienation and unease. However, across time and space, migrants leave their places of birth because they cannot feed themselves or their families or because they cannot lead meaningful lives. "Home" societies did not permit sustainable lives in nineteenth-century Europe and they did not do so in twentieth-century Africa. As one author put it, home may be not only an uninteresting place, it may also be unsafe, unfair, and unjust. A woman from a tradition-fettered community tersely remembered that her society of birth had no fence and no visible exits either. At the destination, receiving or "host" societies may in fact be hostile. Racial criteria – "negro," "redskin," "slit-eye" – may be used to denigrate any migrant of non-white skin colour. Instead of being just one more colour, "white" became a norm imposed by powerful people who could equally well have been described as pale-faced and pigment-deprived.

In addition to labelling by phenotypical skin colour, some societies treat migrant human beings like body parts, commodified as instruments of work: as "hands" or "braceros" (arms) rather than as hearts and heads. In the 1880s, Hawai'ian plantation owners ordered, alphabetically, "fertilizer" and "Filipinos." In Europe after the mid-1950s, recruiting societies wanted nothing but a labour force – "guest workers" – but the guests arrived with emotions, life-plans, and agency. In the early twenty-first century, the term "brain drain migration" also hides the fact that families arrive and that children need playgrounds and schools. Recruiters of body parts never expect "foreigners" to protest inhuman treatment. But migrant men and women generally struggle to make homes in a new society, at least temporarily.

Although oft-repeated, treatment of migrations as the products of "pushes" and "pulls" has been recognized as insufficient to understand migrants in their complexity of culture, gender, class, identification, and intent, and in their moves between complex societies. Scholars now analyze a society of origin in all of its facets to understand the structures and processes which induce or force people to depart. They deconstruct national states into particular regions and localities to clarify migrants' socialization and specific forms of cultural belonging. No generic Chinese settled Manchuria, peopled the Southeast Asian diaspora, or came to the Americas. Rather, specific men and women came from particular regions, different walks of life, several religions, and from urban or rural pursuits. From Africa, no generic slaves were transported to the tropical and subtropical plantation belt: they were Wolof, Ibo, Ashanti, Yoruba, Kongo, who spoke particular languages and lived particular cultures. German speakers who arrived in Canada were German, Austrian, or Swiss, were Catholics, Protestants, or Mennonites, and spoke many, often not mutually intelligible dialects. Without differentiated knowledge of cultures of origin, we easily misunderstand migration decisions, post-migration life-projects, and patterns of acculturation.

How do people travel, once they have decided to depart? Do they leave as individuals or as members of a family economy? Do they move "naturally" because their society expects migration? Does travel involve a few and the charting of a new direction ("pioneer migration") or does it involve many and follow well-established patterns ("mass migration")? Does travel mean a transoceanic passage lasting weeks or a plane ride of a few hours? Does the trip lead migrants across different language and cultural environments? Do people move in groups, like the Huguenots of seventeenth-century Europe or child refugees in the Sudan in the early 2000s? Does migration involve crossing heavily militarized borders such as those of the Rio Grande? Is information readily available? Modern travellers may buy a pocket travel guide book – but ancient travellers also shared knowledge with others: Around 900 CE, ibn Khordadbeh, postmaster of an Arab province in Persia, described land and sea routes as far as Korea in his eight-volume *Book of the Roads and Countries*.

While migrants had to learn to communicate as they travelled to the receiving society, scholars in the past often did not learn migrants' languages. Thus, in the case of the US, they wrote of migrants arriving at Ellis Island with "cultural baggage" but assumed that the men and women simply deposited their baggage at some point. British scholars, writing about contract labourers from colonized India, looked at plantation society conditions and British English-language regulations but did not understand actual living conditions and cultural practices in the South Asian subcontinent's regions of origin. Scholarship thus took up research only in the middle of migrants' lives, truncating human experience.

Without knowledge of migrants' languages, scholars resorted to naturalist-nationalist imagery and posited the "roots" of migrants in their nation of birth. They thus had to invent the "uprootedness" paradigm. Said to possess mental capacities inferior to those of the receiving society and assumed to be torn from their roots by forces beyond their control, migrants were considered adrift or in limbo. But does not a move between societies suggest migrants of keen observation and capability to learn? A late twentieth-century Quiché Indian woman migrating from the Guatemalan highlands to the capital city felt lost – no-one spoke her language and she spoke no Spanish. Likewise, European Jesuits migrating to China's court in the sixteenth century had difficulties in understanding the capital's culture. Both the illiterate peasant women and the educated friars had to learn. Migrants travel with the expectation of learning to live in the new social environment they select or, at least, of finding a niche in which to establish, at first, a narrow base for economic survival. When recognizing these capabilities, scholars substituted the term "transplanted" for "uprooted." Although equally botanical, this image acknowledged human agency, operating in changing societal frames and contexts. Migrants' capabilities are acted out via entryways offered by states and in the receiving society's structures.

Some societies provide open gates, at least for some migrants. Typical were the port cities of the fifteenth-century Indian Ocean's coasts; the littoral societies from East Africa via India's Malabar and Coromandel coasts to Southeast Asia; the Ottoman Empire; and, at the end of the twentieth century, Sweden and the Netherlands, Canada, or Malaysia and Singapore. Other societies – Japan, Uganda, and Germany, for example – have shown hostility to newcomers, although again in very specific ways. It seems that, in some societies, resident "nationals" have little faith in the resilience of their historic culture and see migrants threatening their cultural integrity. Why should a few hundred thousand Korean-origin people in Japan pose a threat to 128 million Japanese, or 2 million Turkish-origin migrants in Germany threaten 80 million culturally German citizens? A similar debate, in the early 2000s, racks the United States of America as regards hardworking migrants from the neighbouring United States of Mexico. With little investment in agriculture in the People's Republic of China, some 120 to 160 million rural labourers have migrated to cities but, at the turn to the twenty-first century, are considered negatively as a "floating population." The narrower the entry gates and the more hostile the reception, the larger the difficulties newcomers face in developing self-supporting and self-determined lives and in contributing to the receiving society.

Worldwide, all societies accommodate in-migrants and all governments have to develop policies if they do not want to depend on erratic stopgap measures. The number of interstate migrants was estimated at almost 200 million in 2006, and the United Nations High Commissioner for Refugees counted some 30 million refugees among them. Far larger numbers, hundreds of millions of men, women, and children, are threatened by environmental degradation, intra-state or inter-state war, oppressive political regimes, or stagnant econo-mies. They are potential migrants – proactive or anticipating ones if they leave voluntarily before disaster hits, reactive ones if they wait until survival becomes impossible. While migration studies provides background for strategic policy-making, migration history emphasizes the continuities and changes of patterns of migration over centuries and millennia.

- Has your family migrated?
- Ask your relatives and neighbours for their migration history. Is there a family memory of migration or do you not recall any mobility in the past or present?
- If you read this text in class, collect the migration histories of students in the class. Indicate the origins of all families on a world map or, if they have migrated within your country, indicate their region of origin. Each student may then select one region of origin of a friend or, alterna-tively, his or her own, and collect information on cultural background(s) to present in class.
- If you moved, "migrated," from your parents' home to your university, discuss your experiences of both regional change and status change from daughter or son in a family to student at a college.

2
Migration in Human History – the Long View[1]

The history of humanity is a history of migration. There was no "pre-history" of unsettled and non-literate peoples followed by the "history proper" of settled empires or nations. Periodization differs between cultural macro- and micro-regions, but we may generalize eight distinct eras of migration over time:

- *Homo sapiens* migration out of East Africa across the world
- migrations in the period of early sedentary agriculture, 15,000–5000 BCE
- differentiation of migrations during urbanization in Mesopotamia, Egypt, the Indic and East Asian societies, and the Mediterranean Phoenician–Hellenistic–Roman World
- migrations from 500 BCE to 1500 CE
- migration, intercultural contact, and trade circuits in the world's macro-regions, 1400–1600
- migration dialectics in colonizer and colonized societies, 1600–1800
- nineteenth-century global migration systems
- twentieth-century migrations.

Our analysis emphasizes intercultural exchanges as well as conflict (when armed in-migrating colonizers forced settled peoples into outbound refugee migrations). It also emphasizes human agency – even forced migrants, such as slaves, leave their mark. Men and women make their history and, collectively, the history of their communities and societies even if under conditions not of their own choosing.

Since early developments cannot be dated precisely, scholars use a "Before the Present" (BP) scale, counting from the year 2000 backward. Since time lines are still being debated, this summary relies on the most plausible interpretations. With the emergence of urban living about 6,000 to 5,000 years ago, archaeological dating becomes far more accurate and is often supported by written records. From this period on, the BP scale is replaced by the widely used "Before the Common Era" (BCE) and the "Common Era" (CE). These are Christian ways of dating, reflecting the secular and imperial power of the Western World after 1500. The year that divides BCE from CE is mere convention since scholars do not agree on the date of the birth of Christ. Other religion-civilizations have different calendars – the Chinese, the Jewish and Muslim calendars, and others. Their starting dates are conventions, too.

2.1 Deep Time: Homo sapiens Migrates from East Africa across the World[2]

About 150,000 to 200,000 years ago, *Homo sapiens*, knowledgeable men and women, emerged in East Africa. Earlier *Homo erectus* and *Homo habilis* (upright walking and tool-making hominids) had developed independently in Africa, China, Southeast Asia, and Europe. *Homo sapiens* were highly mobile accumulators of knowledge. They migrated first across Africa, from 60,000 BCE across the world's tropical zones, and from 40,000 to 15,000 BCE into colder Eurasian and American zones, diversifying into ever more linguistic-cultural groups in the process.[3]

This understanding of humanity in "deep time" has become possible through interdisciplinary research. Archaeologists retrace the emergence and development of tools; linguists model the spread and differentiation of languages; genetic modelling traces ancestral peoples' mixing in particular locations over time. Groups of early human beings are defined as language communities, by genetic similarity or variation, and by tools and pottery. Ethnicities or nations in the modern sense cannot be traced. Once languages and everyday ways of life differentiated through spatial distance, cultural exchanges demanded translators and migration into new ecological environments necessitated adjustment strategies.[4]

Early migrations may be aggregated into six types for heuristic purposes, i.e. to simplify highly complex developments in a plausible manner for easier understanding. Variables for this typology include reasons for departure, establishment of new communities in unsettled areas or by rule over already settled peoples, and duration of stay, as well as degree of mobility.[5]

1   Migration *within a cultural group* that is spread over different geographic locations involves hunting and gathering families and bands, as well as migrations for marriage following matrilinear or patrilinear patterns.
2   Migration of segments of a cultural group into new, unsettled areas is an *outbound branching or filiation migration.*
3   Moves into settled areas which involve establishing rule over the peoples already present are *colonization migrations.* Such *conquest* may involve considerable violence and exploitation or, from the view of those first settled, long-term suffering and oppression.
4   When a group's survival is threatened, conflict with neighbours is becoming destructive, or new living spaces are sought, *whole-community migration* or *migration of peoples* may occur into unsettled regions (as in 2), into settled regions with conquest (as in 3), or with negotiated cohabitation.
5   *Cross-community migration* denotes peaceful and permanent moves or temporary stays ("sojourning") into another group's social space or involuntary transport of slaves or captives into the service of members of a community of different culture.

6 Some peoples, nomads, habitually move during their lives, or by seasons, or because of the very limited resources of their desert or mountainous natural environment. Individuals, for spiritual or economic reasons, may pursue itinerant ways of life – religious teachers or peddlers, for example.

All six types of moves involve men and women; they may also involve children and the elderly. In *Homo sapiens*'s migratory differentiation over time, women's genes and their child-bearing capability played a particularly important role. The dispersions by spatial separation generate cultural change. All migration impacts the group of origin, since the departing men and women take their knowledges and skills, their emotions and spirituality with them. At their destinations, fusion of capabilities, spirituality, and emotions may be innovative, but newcomers may also spread diseases or destroy earlier belief systems, causing havoc. Fusion may lead to "ethnogenesis," the emergence of new peoples; disease and destruction may be genocidal. Epidemics or warfare may weaken people to a degree that they need to migrate to reconstitute viable communities.

Human migration across the world occurred in three major phases. Settlement of the African–Eurasian tropics ended before 60,000 BP. A second phase brought men and women from northeast Africa's Nile Valley and Red Sea littoral to the Arabian peninsula and the South Asian subcontinent. To do so, they needed to develop water's-edge technology, i.e. to learn boating for mobility and to access fish and shellfish as food. Once the "ice age" (130,000 to 20,000 BP) lowered sea levels, peoples also moved on to a subcontinent called Sunda (now the Southeast Asian islands) and, after developing seafaring technologies, they reached Sahul (now the island cluster from New Guinea to Australia) some 40,000 years ago. In the next millennia, with ever more sophisticated navigational techniques, they settled the islands of Near and Far Oceania, as well as Hawai'i (first century CE) and the Easter Islands (*c*.400 CE).[6] Did they reach South America's Pacific coast? While there are no genetic or linguistic traces, archaeological finds of cloth indicate strains of cotton grown in the Indus Valley. Cultural contacts spanned the globe.

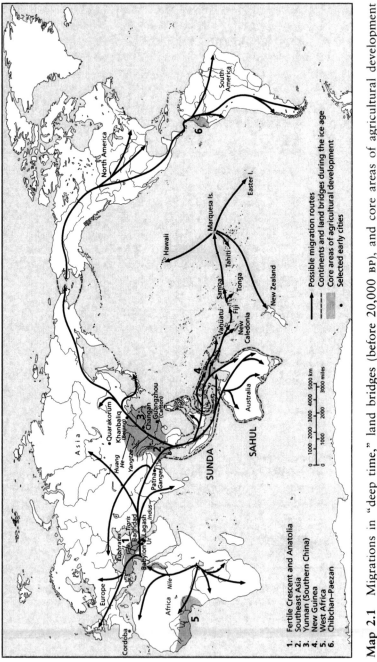

Map 2.1 Migrations in "deep time," land bridges (before 20,000 BP), and core areas of agricultural development (15,000–5,000 BP), and selected major cities (before 1000 CE)

Prepared by Dirk Hoerder from Jeremy Black, *[Dorling Kindersley] World History Atlas* (2000, 2nd ed. London: Dorling Kindersley, 2005), 14–15, 18–19; Rainer F. Buschmann, *Oceans in World History* (Boston: McGraw Hill, 2007), 72.

1. Fertile Crescent and Anatolia
2. Southeast Asia
3. Yunnan (Southern China)
4. New Guinea
5. West Africa
6. Chibchan-Paezan

Possible migration routes
Continents and land bridges during the ice age
Core areas of agricultural development
Selected early cities

Migrants moved toward cooler and drier climates during a third phase, 40,000 to 30,000 BP. Their "land-based cultures" required developing capabilities for storage of gathered vegetables and tools for hunting large mammals. One route went northward from tropical Southeast Asia to Korea and the Japanese isles and westward into the Amur River Valley. A second went westward from the Sino-Tibetan region through the Eurasian steppes to Europe. A third went from the Nile Valley–Fertile Crescent–Black Sea north and through the Caucasus Mountains westward. Moving eastward from Northeast Asia, successive small groups also crossed the dry Bering Strait into the Americas.

2.2 Population Change and Mobility during the "Agricultural Revolution," 15,000–5000 BP

From 15,000 – the end of the last ice age – to about 5000 BP, humans began to understand plant and animal evolution. "Domestication" permitted the transition from natural to culturally developed nourishment: agriculture and horticulture emerged.[7] The two major phases of this "Agricultural Revolution" involved emergent capability to influence plant and animal evolution and inventions, spirituality, and new kinds of sedentary and mobile lives.

From 15,000 to 10,000 BP, some 200 or more generations of humans in six regions of the world experimented with intensive harvesting and new fishing techniques. In the Fertile Crescent from Anatolia to the Nile, people domesticated either cattle or sheep and goats and experimented with grains. In Southeast Asia, Yunnan (southern China), New Guinea, West Africa, and Mesoamerica (regions well watered by rains or rivers), people began to plant and harvest tubers and/or seed-bearing grasses, rice, maize, millet, sorghum, wheat, barley, and other grains. They domesticated squash, bananas, and taro.[8] This new productivity stimulated demand for storage facilities and other craft products, permitted sedentary ways of life, and resulted in higher population growth rates.[9] Uneven population growth set in motion new social dynamics and migrations with characteristics scholars still debate.[10] These migrations did not shift the location of the twelve major language groups already established but did influence the location and survival or expansion of particular groups.

In the second phase of the Agricultural Revolution, migrations re-peopled settled regions through cross-cultural or colonizer contacts. Only marginal regions – the northern sub-Arctic regions, for example – attracted new settlement. During the middle Paleolithic or stone tool period (10,000 BP in the south and 8000 BP in the north) European peoples invented pottery. Their spirituality related to sun and stars. In the Americas, humans learned to hunt Pleistocene mammals, increasing by 8000 BP both food supply and protein intake. From southern China people expanded northward. Africa no longer held the majority of the world's population.

Migrants from agriculturally innovative communities carried new practices, their funds of knowledge, to different language communities and learned from the host community to adjust farming techniques to local conditions. If the in-migrants were numerous and carried prestige, the local community might adopt their language and everyday culture or be colonized by force. If, in contrast, migrants were few but their innovative techniques were attractive, the local community might adopt new practices and absorb the in-migrants. Migrant agency thus transmitted and adapted food-related information and skills, encouraging future population growth.

2.3 Cities, Civilizations, and Seaborne Migrations, c.5000 BCE to 500 CE

Intensification of food production and new migrations increased the exchanges of material culture, and means of transportation diversified. After the development of skin-boats (such as kayaks or canoes) domestication of the donkey in the hills along the Red Sea and of the water buffalo in Southeast Asia gave humans the first pack and draft animals. Around 3000 BCE, domestication of the camel in Arabia and the horse in the Asian steppes as well as the invention of the wheel further increased mobility. Later, the yak in Tibet and the llama in the Andes provided animal power. With these achievements peoples enlarged the distances they could traverse, further differentiating themselves.[11]

Freed from foraging, human labour could be devoted to handicrafts, especially pottery, and to improved, longer-lasting abodes. Life became more sedentary, villages grew, and, perhaps as early as 8000 to 6000 BCE, the first towns emerged in Palestine. Higher productivity could decrease migration since larger populations could be fed; but it could also increase mobility, either through new long-distance trade or because growing populations could no longer be fed locally. Denser populations were more vulnerable to droughts or war, causing involuntary migrations. When settled populations accumulated household goods or wealth, inequalities grew. Rulers sent men as soldiers over larger distances to raid, dislocating people.

Exchanges occurred along roads or waterways, as town names ending in -market, -newmarket, or -ford indicate. Dense commercial connections evolved from about 3000 BCE in the Eastern Mediterranean and Sumerian Worlds (the Fertile Crescent) and in the World of the Southeast Asian islands (connected to South China through the China Seas). Mariners and craftsmen experimented with increasingly sophisticated shipbuilding technologies and navigational techniques until these two macro-regions connected via the Indian Ocean, when sailors decoded the seasonal monsoon winds with their southerly and northerly phases in the first millennium BCE and thus "domesticated" them. The uneven distribution of resources from the Swahili-language cities in East Africa, via Arabia and Persia, to the South Asian port cities and the Malaysian peninsula and Indonesian Islands stimulated exchanges and led to specialized production. In Eurasia, the caravan routes from the Eastern Mediterranean to the Huang He Valley (later known as "the silk road") became safe to travel for merchants. At the western end, the Phoenicians, a generic name for people in sea-trading cities of the Eastern Mediterranean, connected "Orient" – or the western parts of it – and "Occident" even beyond the Iberian peninsula to the tin mines of southern Britain. A Eurasian–North African trading sphere of mobile peoples emerged.

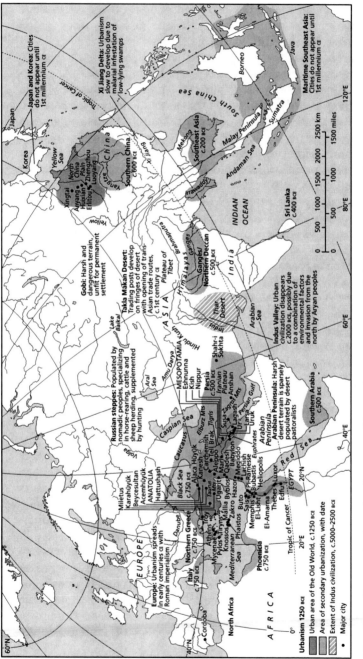

Map 2.2 Zones of urban development, thirteenth century BCE, and their expansion to 0 CE
From Jeremy Black, *[Dorling Kindersley] World History Atlas* (2000, 2nd ed. London: Dorling Kindersley, 2005), 28–29.

According to early writing and pictograms, towns of several thousand existed in Egypt and Mesopotamia after 6000 BCE. By 2000 BCE, the Mesopotamian cities of Lagash and Ur may have accommodated 50,000 and 65,000 inhabitants respectively. By 600 BCE, Babylon had more than 200,000 inhabitants. As Indian Ocean trade increased, so did urban growth. Patna probably became the largest city around 300 BCE and, with the emergence of the Chinese Empire, its capital Changan was also at the top of the list by 200 BCE.[12] Such figures hide high population mobility. People moved in and out of towns and cities depending on their relative position in hemispheric trading systems, on interdynastic warfare, and on the relocation of capital.

Cities needed fresh provisions supplied by men and women from the hinterlands each and every day. Belts of intensive agriculture attracted peasant families as well as male and female labourers. Rural–urban market exchanges intensified. Cities expanded commercial networks and power relations between ruling families, producing intellectual exchanges: scholars travelled to courts; merchants collected geographic and trading information and acquired knowledge about distant social protocols of trade; translators connected cultural regions; newcomers married local women to gain access to knowledge and social networks.

Dense populations and expanding systems of governance required roads and bridges, aqueducts, and new types of sanitation. While unskilled labouring men migrated to build infrastructural earthworks – roads, dykes, dams – women moved to service labour. Brick-making masons replaced mud huts with more durable constructions. In some civilizations, religious customs demanded ritual cleaning, since poor urban sanitary conditions meant high rates of death and constant need for in-migration. Economic sectors and producers' mobility did not end at city walls or political borders.

Exchanges required travel and migration by craftsmen and small and large traders as well as women. Porters, carters, sailors, drivers, as well as translators, money-changers, guards and labour migrants travelled routes to cities. Since labour and reproduction were gendered, men relied on women for key services that included sex and emotional ties. Children of in-migrating single men and resident women might be ostracized as "bastards" or become part of their mother's community.

From the fourth millennium BCE peoples organized themselves or were organized by increasingly powerful elites into a macro-regional hierarchy of urban civilizations: the Sumer (Mesopotamian), Nubian, and Egyptian kingdoms in the Nile and Euphrates–Tigris River valleys, the Persian state, and, in the Indus Valley, the Harappa and Vedic cultures. Around 2000 BCE, in the Northeastern Mediterranean (Crete, Greece, Turkey) the Minoan, Mycenaean, and Hittite societies emerged. Around 1000 BCE, the Phoenician seaborne trading civilization became trans-Mediterranean. The Greek–Egyptian Hellenistic World or, better, World of the Black Athena emerged.[13] A few centuries later, after *c*.500 BCE, it was incorporated into the Roman Empire by mobile soldiers and administered by migrating imperial officials. The Huang He Valley peoples were integrated into the Shang dynasty's realm after 1500 BCE, and the Han dynasties (*c*.200 BCE to 250 CE) enlarged the realm to southern China. Workers were recruited from afar to build the Great Wall to keep out migratory nomadic peoples from Asia's interior. In India, from 500 BCE to 500 CE, the Mauryan and Gupta states controlled large territories and numerous peoples. These civilizations provided integrative structures and new belief systems about society and spiritual realms. But their rulers also engaged in destructive expansionist and inter-imperial warfare. Armed men, commanded to move, in turn sparked civilians' temporary flight and long-term refugee migrations. Although warfare was male, the Roman Empire's founding myth included the abduction of women from a neighbouring people. Despite heroic, usually mythical founding tales, men alone could not turn acts of war into functioning societies. Migration – and violence – is gendered.

The building of ceremonial places, such as pyramids or the later Mayan temples, or the construction of canals (in China) or roads (in Rome), required the mobilization of tens of thousands of labourers. To satisfy demand for labour, powerful rulers bound workers temporarily or enslaved captives for life, forcing them to migrate. Some bound themselves to work off debts; poor families might sell children, often girls, to alleviate their poverty or to save them from starvation.

Cities and towns protected themselves with walls, distinguishing insider from outsider. Migrants, mobile farmers, and merchants asked permission to enter. City gates and the membership category of "citizenship" established formal hurdles. These new legal categories of inclusion or exclusion might be combined with or exacerbated by ascriptions based on language knowledge: the Greek term "barbarian" originally merely designated a person who did not speak Greek, but later it came to imply generic imputed inferiority.[14] "Outsiders" were deemed of lesser culture.

In these urban and imperial societies, new concepts of spirituality emerged and views of the transcendental were said by ruling groups to "mandate" a certain kind of social order. From 800 BCE ethical and reflective thought flourished independently from the Chinese Empire to the Greek city-states: Confucius and Laozi in China, Buddha and the authors of the Upanishads in India, Zarathustra in Persia, the Hebrew prophets in Palestine, and Socrates and Plato in Greece among others. Later, evangelists codified Christian texts and, after 600 CE, propagators of Islam codified the Quran. Spirituality might engender migrations. Several of these spiritual innovators, Loazi and Buddha for example, undertook contemplative pilgrimages; the Hebrews remember their forced migration into bound labour; Muhammad travelled widely as a merchant and fled from Mecca to Medina (*Hijra*) in 622 CE. Religious migrations reflected changes in transport: the Israelites had to walk into captivity, the pregnant Mary was carried by a donkey, and Muhammad could rely on horses and camels. Christian and Islamic missionaries migrated as humble servants of their God, as warrior preachers, or as faithful merchants. Codification and homogenization of old and new belief systems created the three religions "of the book" – Judaism, Christianity, and Islam – but also generated dissent and schisms.

Religious strife and so-called holy wars brought about exile, out-migration, or flight. Spiritual interaction could also generate religio-cultural syntheses and conversion (Bentley). Thus, to the linguistic borderlands of earlier agrarian migrations were added civilizational-dynastic borderlands, zones of exchange and contact, and areas of conflict between religions. New mixed cultures emerged. Whole peoples, such as the

Jews or the Zoroastrians (Parsees), dispersed. Places designated as holy attracted temporary religious migrants, called
pilgrims, from near and far. The change from agrarian to
urban spiritual practices transformed gender relations. Agrarian cults had worshipped fertility goddesses, whereas the
religions of the book centered on male gods, and the original
thinkers of the Persian, Indian, and Sino-Tibetan systems of
thought were also men. Once ingrained in societal norms,
these beliefs were to restrict women's migrations over the
next millennia.

2.4 Migrations and Societies, 500 BCE to 1500 CE

Migrating peoples carried with them "funds of knowledge,"
resources to re-establish themselves at their destination in
different ecological environments. For example, peoples from
northern regions in the Americas moving southward brought
building and sowing techniques that needed to be adapted to
arid conditions to create the cultural space of the pueblos of
Mesoamerican peoples. Competition about spaces or territories often led to neither peaceful resolution nor prolonged
warfare but to asymmetrical, interest-driven and power-
mediated ways of interaction, a "bumping of peoples into
each other." "Many-cultured" complex societies emerged –
we use this term to indicate cultural plurality in the past
without inferring modern multicultural interactions.[15]

   In the Americas, by 10,000 BCE, people of the Chibchan-
Paezan languages (living from southern Mexico to northern
South America) had developed rich agricultural traditions.
Migrating Mesoamerican peoples carried maize to the Adena
and Hopewell mound-builders of the Mississippi Valley
(*c.*700 BCE to 400 CE), which permitted these to become
sedentary. Some people were lost from memory when they
migrated. The "Hohokam," meaning "the people that van-
ished," had once been the Pima's neighbours in North America's southwest. In South American regions with rich fauna
and flora, people could settle without developing agriculture.
In Mesoamerica and Peru a succession of cultural encounters,
state-building, and warfare began at least two millennia

before the Common Era. The Mayan cities in the Yucatan peninsula attracted migrants from 1800 BCE but were abandoned by their inhabitants in the tenth century CE for reasons still unknown. Chichimec migrations (in today's central Mexico) from the eleventh century CE were complex: some entered Toltec urban society and adapted, others migrated but resisted adaptation, and others did not migrate at all. The agricultural and scholarly achievements of the Toltecs, Mixtecs, and Zapotecs (who had migrated southward after 800 CE) provided the base for the fourteenth-century Mexica (Aztec) culture around Tenochtitlan (now Mexico City). Beginning in the ninth century, the Inca Empire on South America's Andean slopes in what is today Peru incorporated neighbouring peoples by conquest, protected people against dislocation by famine, and established postal and messenger systems. This empire required mandatory labour – the construction of Cuzco, for example, employed 40,000 workers seasonally for ten years. Both involuntary resettlement of rebellious populations and voluntary rural–urban moves were an integral part of life in this highly developed and centralized society.

In Africa, the sub-Saharan Khoi and Bantu-speakers moved west- and southward and Nile Valley peoples connected to seafarers of the Mediterranean. Savannah belt peoples migrated westward. In the first millennium CE, historic Ghana connected the Bambuk goldfield through trans-Saharan caravan trading to Morocco. Such routes became more numerous by 900 CE. Islamic merchants from Iberia, from along the Mediterranean littorals, and from northeast Africa migrated southward, initiating conversion. A distinctive form of slavery and unfree mobility also developed. Rich men admitted to their households poor relatives and debtors ("right-in-persons slavery"). Women's labour was so valuable that bound women moved within the region while men were sent farther afield. War captives could be sold in the Mediterranean or, through East African port cities, to societies across the Indian Ocean. In the ports from Sofale (Zimbabwe) to Mogadishu (Somalia), African merchants using Swahili as a commercial *lingua franca* – a widely used language for cross-cultural communication – provided inland connections, Arab speakers provided transoceanic relations, and sailors from as far as the China Seas provided manpower.

Trans-Saharan northward and ocean-borne eastward movements promoted connectivity and cultural *métissage* (mixing).

Peoples in the Mediterranean World also experienced realignments of cultures and religions because of migration. In the northeast, the Macedonian ruler Alexander (336–323 BCE) established rule over Greek city-states, the Persian Empire, and the Indus River region. He marched 35,000 soldiers across Anatolia and into Egypt and dispersed Greek demobilized soldiers into eastern Persia. Refugees fled destroyed cities or were captured and sold into slavery; masons, artisans, and traders migrated individually or as families into newly founded cities; scholars moved to a new center of knowledge in Alexandria. The migrants spread Hellenistic ways of life while absorbing Egyptian and Persian culture and knowledges – essentially converting. In the north-central and northwestern Mediterranean, the Roman Empire and its politics of conquest and incorporation sparked migrations of Greek artisans to Etruscan towns, forced migrations of slaves, and compelled recruitment of soldiers from sub-Saharan and North Africa and Southern Europe. Rome, founded in the eighth century BCE, counted 450,000 inhabitants by 100 CE. Rome's expansion into northern Africa (Carthage) and Iberia (Hispania) brought intermarriage with diverse local peoples. To quell a struggle against misgovernment and for self-rule in Judea (labelled an "uprising" by the Roman governor, himself an administrative migrant), Rome's many-cultured army destroyed Jewish religious institutions. Jews fled first along the Mediterranean littorals and then across Europe. Serving in Rome's armies, African soldiers reached southern Britain and European soldiers reached North Africa. Around 300 CE the empire split into a western part, which absorbed migrant transalpine Germanic peoples, and the eastern Byzantine Empire, which also continued to attract migrants.

After 700 CE, the new Islamic faith expanded through North Africa to the Iberian peninsula. Soldiers, recruited in Palestine, settled as agriculturalists or craftsmen in the Caliphate of Córdoba. Again marriages to local women resulted in ethnogenesis. Islamic Iberia became a tricultural, interreligious Muslim–Jewish–Christian center of learning, building on the legacy of Jewish–Arab–Hellenistic Alexandria in Egypt. Half a million lived in its capital, Córdoba, by the tenth century. Large-scale migrations reversed direction when Frankish Christian armies conquered and destroyed this many-cultured society. By the 1490s, Christian rulers would expel both the Jews (to whom the Ottoman Empire offered asylum) and Muslim artisans and cultivators. The intercultural Mediterranean World came to an end.[16]

In Central Europe, from the fifth century BCE onward, Celtic or Germanic peoples migrated eastward to Asia Minor, northward to Scandinavia, westward to the British Isles, and southwestward into the Iberian peninsula. They settled, conquered, served as support troops for Rome, and "bumped into each other." When the Carolingian Empire emerged around 800 CE, peasants became sedentary, but secular and religious administrators, rulers, and monks migrated in circuits of rule. The successor dynasties of this Central European empire – the so-called Holy Roman Empire – temporarily expanded their rule southward as far as Sicily and northward to Scandinavia. At the top level, emperors spoke Arabic and empresses came from as far as Byzantium. At the bottom level, peasants were bound to their lords and seemingly immobile. Still, some escaped to cities and, if not claimed within a year, became free. Depending on labour needs and agricultural policies, the serf owners sent away others. Medieval European societies, too, were mobile.

In historical imagination, the Scandinavian north and the West-Central Asian steppes have been known as senders of mobile seafaring "Viking" and horse-borne "Mongol" raiders. From the eighth century, Norse peoples with little farmland but much naval experience reached Iceland, Greenland, and "Vinland" in North America. Others crossed the Baltic Sea and Lake Ladoga eastbound, established rule over local peoples along the Dnieper River, and traded with Byzantine, Arab, and Levantine merchants. Still others moved southward, occupied Britain, settled Normandy in France, raided port towns, and established a state in Sicily. Their water's-edge culture combined aggressive manliness with joint male/female migrations. When men moved alone, at their destination they married local high-status women who knew the region's language and culture.

On the Eurasian steppes, mobile horsemen (and, equally, horse-borne women) established aggressively expansive societies and states. From among them, the Arya intruded into northern India and established the Vedic culture from 1500 BCE. In the first millennium CE, steppe peoples moved east, conquered Chinese peasant societies, and took possession of China's imperial government. Warfare between steppe peoples disrupted the "silk road" trade, thereby intensifying the Arab and Gujarati trade in the Indian Ocean. The Khans unsuccessfully attacked Baghdad and its million inhabitants, the capital of the Muslim World. By the thirteenth century, the trans-Asian *pax mongolorum* ("peace of the Mongols") from China to Persia reopened the China–Europe caravan routes. In the early fourteenth century, a migrant clerk from Florence in Italy, earning his living as a trader in the Genoese colony of Kaffa on the Black Sea, compiled a handbook detailing the routes as far as China, with information on resting places and dangerous stretches, on amounts and types of food to carry, and where to exchange money or to engage interpreters. Peoples along the routes learned of distant opportunities from the travelling merchants.

Of the 120,000 foreign merchants said to live in Guangzhou (Canton) in the ninth century CE, some traded as far as East Africa. By the eleventh century, Chinese seafarers had invented the compass, extending trading realms. Living in diasporic trader communities, sojourners initially stayed for the season of one monsoon, then became permanent residents supporting migrations of kinsmen. Under the thirteenth-century Mongol rulers, Khanbaliq (later Beijing) and the capital Qarakorum housed, in addition to Mongols and Chinese, cosmopolitan societies in which numerous Georgians, Armenians, Persians, and Turks mingled with small numbers of Slavs, Hungarians, Greeks, Germans, French, and English. Interfaith contact involved Roman Catholics, Nestorian and Armenian Christians, Buddhists, Jews, and Muslims. Artisans producing luxury goods migrated to the courts and residences of the wealthy; urban men and women went to distant cities; peddlers crisscrossed the countryside; administrators were sent to distant provinces. Recurring natural droughts and floods caused short-term mass migrations and long-term population displacement. Since trade relied on human porters rather than animals, large numbers moved about. The building of irrigation systems for agriculture also demanded workers from afar, and peasants moved to thinly settled regions of the empire.

This was a world of global interactions over great distances. Contemporaries recognized a many-cultured Afro-Eurasian "ecumene" (from Greek *oikos*). Within this space cultural achievements and human beings moved about as much as goods: from China to urban Italy, from the Southeast Asian islands to the Indian Ocean societies, and from the Arabian Seas to the many-cultured Ottoman Empire. The Americas, however, remained separate and unknown to the ecumene's peoples. Mid-fourteenth-century plagues seriously disrupted migration and life in the ecumene. Within a single decade the "Black Death" killed about one-third of the people living in the regions touched. Migrations changed from a search for improved options to resettlement and re-establishment of viable population centers. More than a century passed before families, communities, regional societies, and whole populations recovered from the plagues.

2.5   Two Worlds into One: Migrations, Trading Circuits, and Cultures in Contact, 1400 to 1600

After 1400, two parallel but unrelated developments at the eastern and western ends of the ecumene changed global power relations, bringing the Americas into the worldwide trading and migration pattern and – in the long run – establishing the European and the Atlantic Worlds' predominance. In the East, the Chinese Empire's outward contacts reached their apogee when, from 1405 to 1435, statesman Zheng He voyaged to India, Ceylon, Aden, and perhaps beyond. His ships accommodated up to one thousand passengers; each of his fleets carried about 27,000 men, who even grew fresh vegetables on board. The imperial court, citing both costs and unwanted cultural imports, ended such outreach, but merchants in the distant southern provinces continued to venture out extra-legally. Their diasporic communities in Malacca, Manila, and Batavia included migrating artisans and workers with their families. They traded throughout

Southeast Asia but with no government support, arms, or other defences.

In the West, during the same decades, the crown of tiny Portugal took the opposite course, providing support for merchants to venture outward. Their voyages followed the African coasts southward, reaching first the Atlantic islands and finally West African ports. There the Portuguese built fortified posts and began direct gold trading, thus cutting out the Muslim Arab-controlled trans-Saharan routes. More importantly, local societies provided access to bound, exploitable human labour. At first, merchants exported slaves to the Iberian peninsula as servants and as labourers. As the deadly system of chattel slavery developed, millions of men and women were forced to migrate to the Americas. The Catholic Church sent missionaries along to convert non-Christian or "heathen" peoples, but, since Christianity in its orthodox version was intended to be an exclusive rather than a syncretic religion, earlier belief and value systems were destroyed, weakening their potential for resistance. (Over time, in other regions of the world, Catholicism would incorporate local practices and beliefs.) The Age of Gunpowder Empires – misnamed by Europeans the "Age of Exploration" – and of chattel slavery had begun.[17]

Seafarers from declining Italian port cities on the Mediterranean especially migrated to new opportunities in Iberian seafaring – Columbus, Cabot, Vespucci, and Verranzano among them. Columbus may have visited Icelandic archives to tap the northern migrants' knowledge of "Vinland," but on his westward route across the Atlantic he miscalculated distances and assumed he was in India when he sighted the Caribbean Islands. Travelling a southward route around the tip of Africa that brought him into the Indian Ocean, Vasco da Gama used his guns to force East African cities to reprovision his ships and provide him with pilots to guide his little fleet to India's ports. After 1500, Iberian rulers controlled the Atlantic and Indian oceans. But when they expelled their Jewish communities (unarmed, like the Chinese diaspora), they deprived their empires of experts in long-distance trading. The Urban Netherlands, the Ottoman Empire, and North African societies welcomed the refugee merchants and their funds of knowledge. New fifteenth- and sixteenth-century global power structures replacing peaceful mercantile proto-cols of trade with armed warrior-merchant rule laid the basis for the ascendancy of Europe and the Atlantic World, Asia's relative decline, and Africa's role as labour supplier. These inequalities between macro-regions still influence trade and migrations at the beginning of the twenty-first century.

In the Americas, trading networks and scholarly exchange (astronomy and its religious implications) connected Meso-american cultures. While most people migrated regionally, human porters and itinerant traders covered large distances. The Spanish and Portuguese wars of conquest, their brutal exploitation of Caribbean, Mesoamerican, and Peruvian men, women, and children, and their unwitting introduction of Eurasian pathogens resulted in population collapse. Contact and in-migration were genocidal on several of the Caribbean Islands and near-genocidal in Mesoamerica. The populations of the Mexica and their neighbours declined from perhaps 25 million to some 2 million within a century. Death came less swiftly to dispersed North American and eastern South Amer-ican peoples. As in post-plague Europe, the demographic disaster necessitated new migrations to re-establish viable communities of survivors. Forced relocation of Native Peoples created a labour force for Spanish immigrants. The aggressive Iberian in-migrants (called *conquistadores*) could, if they withstood the climate and courtly intrigues, carry home riches and be honoured as explorer-statesmen. The subsequent "peopling of the Americas" was a re-peopling which occurred after conquest and destruction.

After the "Columbian" exchange introduced domesticated animals into the Americas, some Native Peoples developed horse-borne mobility and hunting cultures. To the Iberian peninsula and to Europe as a whole, returning migrants and royal officials carried food plants and stimulants. In North-western Europe, the potato, in particular, provided a stable food supply that sustained population growth which, by the nineteenth century, compelled millions to depart for the Americas. In Southern Europe, corn and American beans had similar impacts. Sugar, a "migratory crop," carried by mobile cultivators from the Eastern Mediterranean via the Atlantic Islands to the Caribbean, soon became a mass-produced export item that changed Europeans' diets. Further forced migrations from Africa satisfied the plantation regime's demand for labour. Thus the small but powerful Iberian and West European "white Atlantics" brought forth a "black Atlantic." Until the 1830s forced Africans outnumbered European indentured or free migrants to the Americas.

In addition to forcing men and women to migrate in the Afro-Atlantic, the Spanish Iberian migrants established the "*mita*" system of Native People's forced migration and compulsory labour in the Peruvian Andes for high-altitude silver mining in Potosí. With the silver, the Spanish could extend their system of trading goods and human beings globally. Across the Pacific they began the "galleon trade" between Spanish Acapulco (Mexico) and Spanish Manila (Philippines). Spanish and Chinese brought enslaved and free Asian migrants and goods, the latter supplied by the migrants in the Chinese diaspora, to New Spain. Migrating men and women, free and unfree, built the societies and economies of the Americas and Europe. Without their labour no empire could survive. The Iberian nobility's castles reflected the cultural and artisanal capabilities of Muslim men and their families; the Iberians' transpacific ships reflected migrant Chinese ship carpenters' skills.

Two approaches – one cultural, one economic – help to conceptualize interactions in this fifteenth- and sixteenth-century era of globalization. According to Jerry H. Bentley (1993), intercivilizational contact led to "conversion" and to cross-cultural exchange through voluntary association, through political, social, or economic pressure, or through assimilation. In contrast, Immanuel Wallerstein has emphasized economic factors in his "world systems analysis" by which he attempted to explain Europe's post-1500s predominance in global economic and power relations. He argued that gains from capital accumulation accrued mainly to European merchants, investors, and states. Janet Abu-Lughod decentered this perceptive but Eurocentric model by synthesizing the world's pre-1500 "trading circuits" with independent accumulation processes.[18] To such analyses of commodity and capital flows and cultural interaction, the impact of migrations needs to be added as a third factor. Societies and exchanges also change as a result of decisions made by common people.

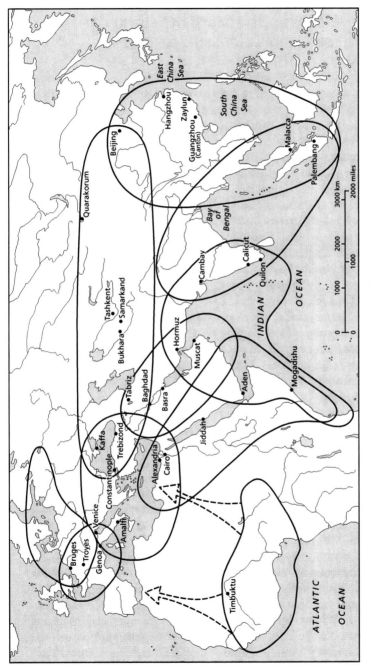

Map 2.3 Circuits of the thirteenth-century Eurasian–African world system: zones of contact, trade, and migration
From Dirk Hoerder, *Cultures in Contact: World Migrations in the Second Millennium* (Durham, N.C.: Duke Univ. Press, 2002), Map 2.2, p. 29.

2.6   People on the Move in Self-Ruled, Colonized, and Colonizer Societies, 1600 to 1800

After a century of sailings across the Atlantic, around Africa, and across the Indian Ocean, the state-supported merchants of Europe had established permanent trading posts in much of West Africa and Asia. Such fortified places of exchange at the end of ship lanes remained quite isolated and interacted little with societies inland. Few Europeans arrived as families, many died of tropical diseases, most needed native "boys" to work for them, and many consorted with colonized women. Only in the Americas did Europeans re-populate whole continents. The decimated people – from the Tehuelche (Patagonians) in the south to the Salish or Beothuk in the north – still outnumbered the enslaved and free Africans (the second-largest group) and Europeans (the smallest but heavily armed and thus most powerful group). Since European migrants were mainly men, they sought emotional comfort and sex from women of other groups. Children were born and yet another process of ethnogenesis began. Labelled inferior to whites, mulattos in Caribbean societies nevertheless became the most influential, for they knew customs and culture as sojourning or in-migrating Europeans did not. Although intent on trade with distant or, at least, resource-rich societies, European merchants had nothing to sell or barter, so they changed the terms of trade with armed bullying and rhetorical appropriation. Silver dug by the forced labour of Peruvian peoples became "Spanish" and spices grown by colonized Southeast Asian island peoples became "Dutch." But even the gunpowder empires had to rely on interpersonal relationships and the transcultural skills and initiative of others. Chinese, Jewish, Armenian, or other merchants, operating without a supportive state, became key mediators.

One example illustrates the braiding together of worldwide trade, local mobilities, and cultural adaptation. Within Asia's societies, merchants traded millions of pieces of Chinese porcelain. When demand from Europe's commercial migrants increased, Chinese entrepreneurs increased imports of the fashionable "Muhammadan blue" colour from Central Asia and marketed these high-quality products in Dutch Batavia (Jakarta). Shipping 3 million pieces of Chinese porcelain to the Netherlands between 1602 and 1657, and almost 200,000 pieces of Japanese porcelain in the twenty-five years after 1650, required thousands of mobile sailors, carriers, packers, wagoners, and their families. These expensive pieces of "china" became showpieces in Europe's wealthy households; migrant female servants then spread the taste for such items to low-income people. Sensing an opportunity, eighteenth-century potters in the Dutch city of Delft imitated the blue-and-white style and found a ready mass market. The inexpensive "Chinoiserie" even came to be considered "typically Dutch." Consumers thus Europeanized the origins of their new material culture, rendering invisible the ingenuity of distant producing families as well as the mobility and fusion involved. Migration thus had led to Asia–Europe cultural contact and to intercultural imports which, incorporated into everyday household life, changed Europe's material culture.

In Asia, the land-centered Chinese Empire, the Japanese islands, the Southeast Asian societies, and the peoples of South Asia remained separate cultural macro-regions because of physical geography.[19] All were subdivided regionally: China's southern provinces became regions of emigration to the Southeast Asian islands, while people further north engaged in intra-empire migrations. In India and in China – as in Europe – people migrated to territories depopulated by warfare or disease, or that were more thinly settled or more difficult to till. Regardless of culture or location, each peasant family with more than two surviving children needed additional land, making peasantries mobile in Tokugawa Japan and Georgian England.[20] Social ecologies framed migration strategies: whole families departed if means permitted. Some children migrated to marginal regions nearby or to more distant fertile lands, frequently displacing previous inhabitants upon arrival, whether in North America or Manchuria. Alternatively, some family members migrated to labour markets in the next town or across an ocean. Their remittances sustained kin at "home" where land was insufficient for survival. Given the gendered division of labour, young women moved into service positions rather than into artisanal or other production.

Just as China and Portugal reached different decisions about trade and power, a third change of global impact occurred in the "hinge region" between the Indian Ocean cultures, the Central Asian migration and trade routes, and the Mediterranean and Atlantic Europe. By the mid-fifteenth century, the Muslim Ottoman Empire replaced Christian Byzantium. Its imperial institutions were innovative but resembled those of port cities, where a "neutral" state governed many peoples, cultures, and religions. Peoples defined by religion and ethnoculture (*millet*) administered themselves, with non-Muslims paying an additional but not oppressive tax. To develop underpopulated regions, Ottoman authorities resettled families involuntarily (*sürgün*) but offered such attractive conditions that kin and friends from their region of origin usually followed voluntarily. To avoid ethnocratic rule (which became the principle in nation-states), the imperial court's women, including the sultan's wife, were chosen from highly educated Central Asian or Eastern Mediterranean slave women and the imperial administration used an artificial language (*lingua nullius*). Its core army consisted of slave soldiers recruited afar, while its top executives were Islamicized and educated Christians levied as children by draft from their families. The warrior-founders' Turkish ways of life, religion, and language thus did not threaten interfaith and inter-ethnic coexistence. The empire attracted refugees with human and social capital, such as the Iberian Jews. It provided a model of a non-ethnic state that allowed structural accommodation for people of many cultures and religions.

When Christian Europe divided itself into Catholic, Protestant or Reformed, and many smaller confessions, religious strife generated refugees. The Thirty Years' or First European War (1618–48) left one-third of Central Europe's population dead; whole regions needed in-migrants to regain socio-economic viability. Huguenots (Reformed Protestant refugees from Catholic France) carried their entrepreneurial and mercantile knowledge to other Protestant societies. Puritans, from England, fled first to the Protestant Netherlands, then to North America. Culturally unprepared, they had to rely on Native Peoples to survive. Intra-European migrations of religious refugees, rural–urban, inter-urban, or of peasants in search of land or wages, surpassed the long-distance migrations to the South Russian plains or to the Americas. In relation to population, Dutch migration levels were higher in the seventeenth century, at the apogee of colonizing outreach, than in the twentieth century. In mid-seventeenth-century Europe, several long-term migration regions emerged. The Netherlands became the center of attraction in the North Sea system; central Spain attracted labour migrants from south-central France (mostly single men who married locally); and the Baltic Sea's littoral societies attracted migrants of many trades and skills. Agrarian migrants headed to the South Russian plains and to urban labour markets.

In the Americas, migrations of Native (or First) Peoples had involved continual peaceful economic exchanges and inter-tribal wars. With the arrival of Europeans, northern mobile or sedentary societies supplied the fur for a trade financed in London–Amsterdam–Paris–Moscow and extending northward and eastward to Scandinavia and Siberia. A circum-global northern fur trading sphere emerged. Meso-american societies, decimated and weakened, were unable to survive independently and were relocated against their will. First Peoples and African slave men and women, as well as European-origin colonizer elites, fused into new sixteenth- and seventeenth-century societies in the Caribbean, New Spain, and Portuguese Brazil. In North America, migrants from New Spain (modern Mexico) arrived in Florida and New Mexico; Catholic French migrants went to the Carolinas and the Saint Lawrence and Mississippi valleys. The anglophone Puritans, who credited themselves with pioneering the settlement, arrived late. Religious refugees from intolerant European states settled Maryland and Pennsylvania; Irish men and women fled English colonial rule, while Scottish Highland crofter families were displaced by their own upper classes, who deprived them of their sustenance-producing family plots for the new economy of sheep raising. Most of Europe's poor could not afford the cost of the transatlantic voyage. They sold their labour for three to seven years to ship captains, who then sold them as indentured labourers in the mainland and Caribbean colonies. The Protestant English-speaking migrants of "New England" later expunged such diversity from historiography and memory.

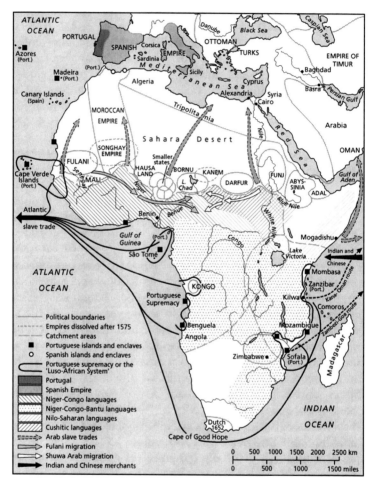

Map 2.4   African trade and migration around 1600 CE
From Dirk Hoerder, *Cultures in Contact: World Migrations in the Second Millennium* (Durham, N.C.: Duke Univ. Press, 2002), Map 6.3, p. 147.

The involuntary Africa–Americas migrations involved some 12.4 million transported men and women. Almost 2 million failed to survive the inhuman conditions of the Middle Passage.[21] In Africa's societies, deaths by raids and forced marches to coastal or desert-edge depots were higher still. African-origin men and women re-created some of their customs in societies such as Brazil, with its high percentage of enslaved, manumitted, and free Africans or "mulattos" (offspring of white–black unions and rape). In the US, by contrast, generic slave cultures emerged among people from many different cultures who, often, had survived an intermediate sojourn – called a "breaking-in" period – on Caribbean plantations.

Many of these migrations were related: Europe's ascendancy set off outbound colonizer migrations; upon arrival merchants set in motion local producer and trader migrations; migrant imperial civil and military personnel controlled and moved colonized people; and investor migrants imposed slave and indentured migrations for their plantations or mines – sometimes called "extractive industries." By the eighteenth century, a plantation belt circled the subtropical and tropical regions of the world. The dialectic of European colonizers' investments and regimes of forced labour involved involuntary mobilization of men and women in less well-armed societies as well as immobilization through bondage after transport. Self-determined migration of peasant families colonized land and expelled prior residents in the Americas, Australia, South Africa, and elsewhere. Globally, region-specific rural and urban migrations continued alongside long-distance and colonizer out- or in-migrations. For example, in many farming regions – villages in India, in Swiss mountain valleys, in New England's rural settlements – women and men had been active in the production of cloth or of refined labour-intensive goods, such as lace, in winter, when no agricultural tasks occupied them. Concentration of such production in "manufactories" (using hand rather than machine production) forced many of the underemployed rural producers to migrate to these emerging centers. Out of these "proto-industrial" migrations, the nineteenth-century proletarian mass migrations would develop.

2.7 Global Migration Systems in the Nineteenth Century

Four major migrations systems operated across the globe in the nineteenth century. From Europe outward *the Atlantic migration system* expanded after 1815, stagnated after the

1920s, and ended in the 1950s. The *Afro-Atlantic slave and forced labour system*, initiated in the 1440s, lasted until the 1870s. When planters anticipated post-slavery labour shortages, imperial authorities imposed a *system of indentured or contract labour migration* on Asian societies from the 1830s until the 1920s/1930s. A *continental system of multiple migrations* stretching from European to Siberian Russia emerged in the 1820s, changed in the 1930s, and ended as late as the 1950s. The vast majority of people moving in these systems were labour migrants.[22]

The Atlantic migration system is the best studied. Europe's second major war after the Thirty Years' War, the revolutionary and anti-revolutionary campaigns after 1792 and Napoleonic-imperial warfare after 1798, mobilized more than a million soldiers, uprooted millions of men, women, and children as refugees, and discarded wounded and exhausted soldiers far from their birthplaces in a region extending from Paris to Moscow and from Italy to East Prussia. Coincidental with the re-establishment of a reactionary trans-European regime in 1815, the famine winter of 1816–17 forced Central European peasant families from the southwestern German-language region to resume their eighteenth-century emigrations. Their traditional route down the Danube to the South Russian plains, however, was being closed, as tsarist authorities privileged migrants of Slavic language and culture. Thus families increasingly travelled westward down the Rhine to Dutch ports and Atlantic ships. In the course of the century this route became the most common choice of Western, then Northern, and finally Eastern and Southern Europeans. Other migrations from Atlantic Europe targeted agricultural settler colonies in Algeria, South Africa, Kenya, and Australia, or – in small numbers – plantation colonies in the Caribbean, South Asia, the Southeast Asian islands, or elsewhere. While the world's population grew by about 60 percent in the nineteenth century, Europe's population doubled between 1815 and the 1930s, despite an emigration of an estimated 55 million.

Until the 1850s, one-third of the US-bound men and women migrated to farms but, after 1890, 95 percent took up industrial labour. Without this "proletarian mass migration" the US transition to urban-industrial production could not have taken place. Likewise, without the US-specific division of tasks into skilled and unskilled, rural Europeans could not have found jobs. Racism led the US to exclude migrants from Asia beginning in the 1880s and people of "olive" or "swarthy" South European and "dark" Slavic "stock" after 1921. Canada, which admitted migrants through the 1920s, continued to attract agriculturalists. Parallel to the North Atlantic route, millions moved from the Iberian and Italian peninsulas to South America, where by 1826 most colonies had achieved independence. Frontier societies such as Brazil were attractive, although most migrants became plantation workers. After 1890, agriculturally knowledgeable but industrially unskilled Italian migrants integrated the southern and northern routes, choosing destinations that ranged from Buenos Aires to New York and Montreal. About one-half of these "immigrants" returned to Europe; they had come as sojourners or "guest workers."[23]

The Afro-Atlantic slave and forced labour system, or "black Atlantic," seemed about to end when the British Empire and the United States, embracing new human rights concepts promoted by black and white abolitionists, prohibited the slave trade in 1807/8. (Other European powers followed in 1815.)[24] But neither European slave traders, nor African slave suppliers, nor Euro-colonial planter classes respected the law. White plantation owners experimented with replacement labour in the form of impoverished European (white) workers or Asian (yellow or brown) workers, but also brought 2 million more Africans to the Americas before 1880. Slaves in French Saint Domingue, in 1794–1804, freed themselves, and some of the refugee planters formed a French-language community in New Orleans. Abolition of slavery itself came in the 1830s in British colonies and elsewhere still later.

Few free or freed African-origin Americans returned to Africa. In the United States, abolition came in 1863–5, two years after autocratic Russia abolished serfdom. Advocates of a whites-only society encouraged the migration of emancipated slaves to Liberia and Sierra Leone. In the mixed societies of Brazil and Cuba, where slavery ended only in the 1880s, transculturation processes differed from those in the segregated Protestant United States. Free African-origin people in the Americas migrated internally to regions where they could either farm independently or enter wage labour outside the oppressive plantation regime. Employers' unwillingness to provide humane or well-paid working conditions, and the resulting dispersal of the liberated labour force, retarded economic development. In the US, racist controls delayed out-migration from the southern states for half a century but, in the absence of entrepreneurial capital and expertise, no development occurred there either.

The continued demand for tropical foods by consumers in the white Atlantic kept the demand for bound labour high. At the same time, European powers and the US engaged in opening Asia's markets to their exports. With its 1840–42 war, the British Empire, acting as a drug-dealer cartel, forced the opium trade on the Chinese Empire. Drug consumption produced impoverishment, which increased migratory potential and associated the Chinese with an "opium den" image worldwide. In Japan, the US navy forced the ruling dynasty to accept Western trade in 1853. The new ruling elites' program of industrial modernization, funded through heavy taxation of the peasantry, forced many young people from Japan's rural regions to emigrate. In India, ruled by the private East India Company with the support of tax-funded armies, a struggle – "mutiny" in British terminology – to oust the colonizers in 1858 was unsuccessful.

As a post-slavery reservoir of labour that was neither free nor bound for life, male and female workers in India and China were mobilized for work in Europe's empires. Men, recruited for the plantation belt that stretched from Mauritius via Natal to the Caribbean societies, bound themselves for five years, sometimes with a guarantee of return, sometimes with the option of reindenture, or sometimes with enforced involuntary contract extension. In India, British authorities demanded that one-third of the migrants be women. Imperial "protectors" notwithstanding, this "second slavery" imposed brutal working conditions on "coolies."[25] In China, local recruiters sent working men to plantations and mines. Far larger numbers migrated under a system of buying tickets on credit and working off their debt or even with funds saved prior to departure. To supply their bound countrymen and -women with culture-specific foods and other items, or to take advantage of opportunities elsewhere, free "passenger" migrants set up businesses. The presence of women among them permitted establishment of communities, and free migrants became politically active in receiving societies in South and East Africa, the Caribbean, Australia, and Hawai'i, and along the Peruvian and California coasts. During World War I, hundreds of thousands of "colonial auxiliaries" laboured for British and French troops in Europe. Some settled there, others joined anti-colonizer struggles; India's nationalist politicians, in return, negotiated the abolition of contract labour. In size (48 to 52 million), these migrations were similar to the European ones, but a far higher percentage of the migrants returned to their societies of origin.

Workers and rural settlers created the Russo-Siberian migration system. Its origins lay in Russia's competition with China along the Amur River, which involved sending troops and supportive personnel, in the deportation of criminals and political opponents to exile in Siberia, and in perceived economic opportunities in these regions, as well as in tillable, thinly settled land which attracted voluntary migrants and entrepreneurs, but mostly peasants. Altogether, however, these were at first numerically small eastbound migrations from European Russia.[26] Since the lands of southern Siberia were fertile as well as distant from government tax-collectors, enserfed Russian peasants also migrated unofficially eastward. In European Russia, where the communal character of village organization made individual out-migration difficult even after the end of serfdom in 1861, ever more men, as well as some women – 13 million in the decade after emancipation – migrated to industrializing cities. (In contrast, in the US, lynching and other controls prevented comparable moves by freed African Americans.) The "central industrial region" of Moscow and St Petersburg and the southern Donbass and Urals mining and industrial belt received the bulk of the migrants. By 1900, more than 70 percent of Moscow's and St Petersburg's inhabitants were migrants. Russia's migration system remained largely separate from the transatlantic system. However, small numbers of West and Central European experts and skilled craftsmen migrated east into Russia. After the 1880s, economic oppression of and pogroms against

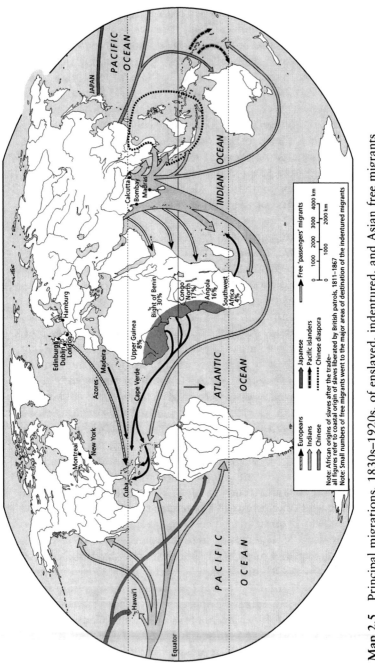

Map 2.5 Principal migrations, 1830s–1920s, of enslaved, indentured, and Asian free migrants
From Dirk Hoerder, *Cultures in Contact: World Migrations in the Second Millennium* (Durham, N.C.: Duke Univ. Press, 2002), Map 15.1, p. 368.

Jews, ethnic oppression of Ukrainians, and withdrawal of privileges once granted to Mennonite and other German-speaking agriculturalists forced these groups to migrate from tsarist Russia to cities in Europe and North America.

Students of transatlantic migrations long considered these the largest in the world, but comparative assessment of quantitative data yields more complex results. In the Russo-Siberian system (including the trans-Caspian region) 10 to 20 million men and women moved in the century before 1914. The Atlantic migration system involved some 50 to 55 million between the 1820s and the 1930s, while the Asian system involved approximately 42 to 48 million Indians and southern Chinese as well as Pacific Islanders in small numbers. The vast majority of Indians moved to British-ruled Burma. A further system, beginning only in the late nineteenth century and lasting to the 1940s, brought some 46 to 51 million men and women from northeastern China to Manchuria as well as from several origins to Japan. About 1 million Asian migrants participated in the Pacific migration system's second phase from the 1840s to exclusion in 1882 from the United States and in the 1930s from Latin societies in the Americas.[27] Everywhere, more people moved internally than across borders or oceans.

By the end of the nineteenth century the global economic consequences of earlier migrations had accelerated departure rates. Migrants had settled the vast plains in North America, South Russia, Argentina, and Australia and begun mass production of grain. With the mechanization of harvesting in these regions, world market grain prices collapsed. In the regions from which they came, small and undercapitalized family farms in hilly regions, in which mechanization of harvesting was difficult, could no longer sell their limited surpluses, and the children of rural families had to seek distant wage work to support their deficit-producing "homes" by remittances. In the US, the mythologized westward migrations were surpassed in volume by eastward migrations of the sons and daughters of farming families to industrial jobs and urban amenities.

Most migrants never expected "unlimited opportunities." In their own words, they moved "to bread" and they expected to work hard for it. Asian-origin plantation labourers in

Hawai'i and European workers in Brazil's coffee plantations or North America's industries complained that draft animals at home were treated better than labouring men and women in the factories and fields. Such migrants, bound or self-willed, from and in all segments of the globe, exploited or seizing options, built the urban and industrialized Worlds that had came into being at the turn to the twentieth century. Those in the plantation belt fed both migrants and residents in the North Atlantic region as well as elsewhere in the world.

2.8 Refugee-Generation, Unmixing of Peoples, and Forced Labour Migrations in the First Half of the Twentieth Century

Nation-states reached their apogee between 1880 and 1920 – a less than analytical assertion in scholarship, since much of Europe was still under the control of the Habsburg, Hohenzollern, Romanov, and Ottoman dynasties, while the Windsors took over from the Hanoverian dynasty and ruled over English, Scots, Welsh, and Irish, as well as over the largest colonial empire ever amassed. The republican French state also ruled colonies, as did a number of smaller states, most destructively Belgium in Congo. The US annexed Spain's possessions in Puerto Rico and the Philippines, interfered with Cuba, and militarily occupied Caribbean states, but elsewhere pursued a strategy of "informal empire" through cultural-religious and economic ("dollar diplomacy") hegemony rather than political-territorial rule. When authorities in the many-cultured Habsburg, Romanov, and Ottoman empires imposed Austrian-German, Russian, and Turkish national dominance, the "lesser peoples" in their realms began to demand cultural autonomy and political self-rule. After 1880, anti-imperial movements grew.

   In nineteenth-century Europe, the middle classes' new ethnocultural consciousness had contributed to unifying nations and nation-states. Nationalism became aggressive; unconditional adherence to "the nation" became a virtue. Under dynastic regimes, migrants had negotiated their status with the ruler of the society of destination, and they could "belong" by swearing allegiance. Under nation-state regimes, and with, by the 1880s, the introduction of citizenship and passport legislation, entry regulations became far more restrictive and demands for loyalty and military service to the nation increased. To belong, migrants – and resident minorities – had to change cultures, to "assimilate" to the ways of life of the host or hostile society, and "naturalize" – as if people of other cultures were not "natural." "Assimilation" required unconditional surrender of pre-migration ways of life. The presence of migrants and resident "minorities" was said to threaten national homogeneity. The cultural repression by some states of migrant communities and historic, now marginalized "minorities" sent the latter into migrations to societies in the Americas. Non-national peoples might be deemed inferior and, if the inferiority was constructed as a genetic defect, they were labelled as unassimilable races.

The Austro-Hungarian Empire's refusal to grant independence to people deemed "non-national" resulted in World War I (1914–18). While the war itself generated millions of refugees, the new post-war nation-states, driven by the ideology of homogeneity of nations, initiated programs of "unmixing" of peoples, or "ethnic cleansing." The "body" of the nation was to be free from alien, sometimes considered "parasitic," bodies feeding on the blood of the nation. In the many-cultured Balkan and Germanic-Slavic regions, hundreds of thousands of families and individuals were denied belonging and were deported or resettled.

After World War I, movements across the globe were no longer dominated by labour migrants. In northern China, the high-volume rural and urban migrations to Manchuria continued. Among colonized peoples, demands for self-rule gained ground. Students' migration from India to Great Britain and from West Africa and the Caribbean to France resulted in new intercultural dynamics. Invited to absorb colonizer cultures, students experienced discrimination and racism. In consequence, they critiqued the colonizers' rhetoric of "imperial citizenship," "*enfants de la patrie*," and "mother countries." Recognizing the equal value of European and African, and of white and black cultures, students from Senegal and Martinique in France called for cultural fusion, "*négritude*," in the 1930s. A few colonial West African labourers found jobs in southern France, and Chinese and Indian sailors, "lascars," lived in London and other European port cities. They were uneasily tolerated but marginalized by the white host societies.

In Asia, after 1900, Japan's elites began an aggressive expansion into Korea, then into Manchuria and China, and finally into much of East and Southeast Asia. By the late 1930s, 100 million Chinese refugees fled the advancing armies, while the colonized Koreans laboured for the occupier. When advocates of Nazi ideology (based on Aryan superiority) took over the state in Germany, they began deportation of German Jews as well as of Gypsies and others. European Jews, managing to escape the Holocaust, migrated to Palestine – the origin of their and others' religions. The wars of Jewish refugees with Arab states, in turn, forced resident Palestinian people to flee. At the beginning of the twenty-first century, many still live in camps.

After 1910, many states of the North Atlantic World no longer required additional industrial workers; exceptions were France and Canada (as well as Australia). In the US, internal regional disparities between labour supply and demand led to African-American mass migrations from the South to jobs in northern cities' industries. When, in the 1940s, US men were drafted into the army, an agreement with Mexico brought millions of replacement workers, "braceros," into the US, a migration that continued after the war. During the Great Depression in the 1930s, only Russia and Germany needed in-migrating workers in large numbers. The new socialist Soviet Union, recovering from both war and civil war, needed to reconstruct cities and industries. Under Stalin, the state resorted to harsh labour regimentation from the 1930s and on forced migrations to new industrial sites. Peasant families fled from collectivization of agriculture; the consequent production collapse led to famine-induced mass migrations. In war-ravaged Germany, the Nazi regime's preparation for further war drafted young people into the labour force and moved them about. As Germany occupied other countries after the beginning of World War II in 1939, it deported 11 million men, women, and – sometimes – children to labour camps. Following Germany's defeat in 1945, 7 million "displaced persons" emerged from these

labour camps and a few hundred thousand from the extermination camps. The Return of the wartime masses of refugees,
repatriation of prisoners of war, migrations from and to
destroyed cities, emigration of displaced persons, and flight
from new communist regimes in East Central European states
kept mobility high.[28]

In the first half of the twentieth century, Europe's nation-
states and the new Eastern Mediterranean country of Turkey
generated millions of refugees. In warfare, the imperial
powers had destroyed their own economic and power potential. Colonial labourers were used to support the war efforts
while colonial students questioned white rule. The Japanese
state copied European models, turned imperialist, and – under
the guise of forming a Greater Asia Co-Prosperity Sphere to
assist Asian people in liberating themselves from Europeans'
colonial rule – extended warfare and refugee generation to
East Asia.

2.9 Decolonization and New Global Patterns of Migration since the 1950s

In the second half of the twentieth century, decolonization
and the continuing imposition of global terms of trade on the
decolonized southern hemisphere by the former colonizer or
indirect rulers in the "North" shifted refugee and labour
migrations to the "South." The "Western" countries, which
had sent migrants – often armed – out to all other parts of
the world, now became the destination of unarmed, often
desperately poor migrants. Militarized border controls proved
ineffective when imposed.

The Atlantic World's imperialist states did not seize the
opportunity of Europe's decline and the defeat of Japan in
1945 to negotiate an end to colonialism. After struggling for
a political route to independence, peoples in the populous
colonies of Asia, especially Dutch Indonesia and French Indochina, as well as in North and sub-Saharan Africa, began
wars for independence. By the 1960s they had forced Britain,
France, the Netherlands, Italy, and Belgium to relinquish
most of their colonies worldwide, while Portugal held out

into the mid-1970s. In addition to refugee movements, three major types of migration ensued: "reverse migrations" bringing colonizers and their personnel back to the metropoles, "displacement migrations" as a result of the reordering of societies within the newly independent states, and income-generating labour migrations abroad offsetting the disruptions of daily lives and of long-term prospects in the newly independent states. An emerging North–South divide, institutionalized through unequal terms of trade that favoured the industrialized and powerful North, continued earlier forms of more direct exploitation and guaranteed continuing migrations. This North–South divide, often called hemispheric, in fact divides the world geographically along the shores of the Mediterranean and the Caribbean: it pits one-sixth to one-quarter of the global population (living in the European Union and in North America) against the other three-quarters or more.

Decolonization ended the temporary assignments of administrators and soldiers in colonies of exploitation and the privileged position of long-term settler families in colonies of agricultural settlement. Many chose "reverse migration," as they saw their political power crumble, their economic calculations collapse, their lifestyles vanish, and "their" subaltern Native labour rise to citizenship. Since most were locally born "creoles," who had never known the society of origin, their flight was not "return" migration. The departure of colonizer elites, with their capital, skills, and knowledge, could and did create havoc in the economies of the new nations. Colonial auxiliaries of the empires, often used to police their co-ethnics, had to leave: the *harki* were locally recruited in French Algeria, the Sikhs were distributed across the British Empire, the Hmong in Indochina supported US warfare against majority populations. Men, women, and children of genetically mixed ancestry, as well as elites with cultural affinity to the colonizers, found themselves in a precarious position, but colonizer states showed no willingness to protect their erstwhile allies or to permit them to migrate to the "mother country." The arrival of some 5.5 to 8.5 million Italian, French, British, Belgian, Dutch, and other white colonials and non-white auxiliaries in Europe before 1975 caused hostility. Taxpayers saw no reason why they should support settler and planter "returnees" who had never lived in the country. Mixed-origin families and their children faced racism, while "coloured" auxiliaries who were, in fact, transported to the former colonizer society often ended up marginalized in camps or substandard housing.

Displacement migrations began after liberation when, first, some of the newly independent states "unmixed" peoples by ethnic or religious affiliation – as, for example, in the division of British India in 1947 into a predominantly Hindu India and a predominantly Muslim Pakistan. The unwillingness of religious-political leaders to develop an interreligious state produced 4 million refugees. Second, in some states dominant majorities or ruling elites displaced immigrant minorities. South Asians, for example, were expelled from Kenya and Uganda in the early 1970s. As in Europe's nation-states, such minorities were said to undercut the new states' "national" homogeneity. Thus Tamils in Ceylon/Sri Lanka were "repatriated" to southern India where their ancestors had originated generations ago. A third issue involved status or class. In China and Vietnam, for example, landowners were deported. This ideologically motivated recomposition of society followed an economic rationale, since structural changes in agriculture – just as in Europe and North America a few decades earlier – demanded larger production units and forced families off their lands. Policy- and persecution-induced mass departures resulted in further severe disruptions of socio-economic structures.

Out-migrations did not end with departures of colonizer personnel. Dysfunctional governing systems in some of the new states resulted in loss by emigration of the educated and the economically active. New (male) elites in the decolonized societies often did not achieve consensus: some former forces of national liberation established single-party rule, clans or dictators exploited the new states' resources for their own purposes, warlord destruction and plundering sent whole populations fleeing, civil war between ethnocultural and ethno-religious segments of populations or religious and ideological fundamentalism deprived whole populations of options for sustainable lives. They, too, tried to emigrate. Most post-colonial migrants decided to move to the wealthier former colonizer countries with which, after generations of rule, they shared language and structural practices. Subsequent and even larger migrations resulted from what might be called recolonization through the unequal terms of trade imposed by the powerful industrial states. The North–South divide as a kind of "global apartheid" is manifest in the data of the UN *Human Development Report* and the World Bank of 1995: the average annual per capita Gross National Product (GNP) of US$380 in low-income countries compared to US$23,090 in high-income economies.[29] Because of cultural affinities, there is no immediate correlation between income differentials and interstate migration, but ever more people did attempt to reach the job-providing, wealthy North, with or without official documents. Poor villagers in Senegal, for example, know that in Paris and London street cleaners are paid wages to pick up dog droppings. Aware that they can do better than that, they assume such wealthy societies will provide options and jobs. Similarly, Chinese in the investment-deprived countryside know that the fast-growing urban labour markets in the country provide more options. By 2005, some 160 million were on the move – labelled by authorities as an unstable "floating" population rather than a hardworking class of migrants.

Across the globe, eight macro-regional overlapping migration systems emerged. The Atlantic migration system ended in the mid-1950s and two South–North systems developed in its place in Europe and North America. Western Europe's population, reduced by tens of millions in the warfare of 1939–1945, drew several million East European German-origin refugees and expellees, displaced persons, and reverse colonial migrants. By the early 1950s, post-war reconstruction and economic growth created demand for labour. A new migration system from Southern to Western and Northern Europe emerged in the mid-1950s and expanded into North Africa in the 1960s. Migrants were called "guest workers," since they were expected to return to their societies of origin. The working guests, however, pursued their own strategies: they brought kin, formed families, and settled. By 2000, they accounted for approximately 8 to 10 percent of the population of the receiving societies. A parallel South–North migration system developed in anglophone and francophone North America. Mexicans and, later, migrants from other Latin

American and Caribbean societies moved north. Demand for labour as well as professionals remained high and, in the 1960s, Canada and the US replaced admission criteria based on race with merit systems based on skills and capabilities. Since then migrants have arrived from some 180 cultures across the globe, and large-scale transpacific in-migration from Asian societies in particular brought well-educated families and business people.

A third system of regional migrations systems developed in the Caribbean and Central and South America. The position of Latin American societies in the global system of inequalities as well as the limited investment strategies of these societies' elites created gaps between labour supply and job availability. From Mexico (since the late nineteenth century) and the Caribbean (since the 1910s) people travelled north, often as US capital investments transformed their societies. In the 1970s and 1980s, right-wing governments, supported by some US administrations, generated large refugee movements. After a US-supported coup against President Allende in 1973, Chilean democrats, for example, had to leave and were forced to establish a North American–European diaspora. In contrast, Venezuela, Argentina, and, most recently, Brazil are becoming centers of attraction in this hemispheric migration region, and political refugees from the military dictatorships have been returning after the re-establishment of lawful governments.

In Asia, a new fourth regional system links the fast-growing economies of South Korea, Singapore, and Malaysia. In contrast, the historic Chinese diaspora in Southeast Asia, after the end of colonial rule, faced increasingly nationalist host societies. These migrants were singled out as scapegoats for economic problems and, after the 1949 establishment of the communist People's Republic of China, often accused of being communist agents. Hundreds of thousands departed under duress or were forced to flee. Japan, pursuing its continuously racist policies, did not admit immigrants, demand for labour notwithstanding, and its Korean labouring population (from colonial times) experiences discrimination.

This intra-Asian system was supplemented by the third phase of the Pacific migration system, which developed after the end of race-based exclusion criteria in North America.

Men and women from the three Chinas – the People's Republic, Hong Kong, and Taiwan – and from India, the Philippines, and Southeast Asia moved to the US and Canada and, in smaller numbers, to those European societies to which colonial ties had existed.

The booming oil-extracting economies of the Persian Gulf region created a sixth new center of labour force attraction that recruits experts from the Western World and male workers from Arab North Africa and the Indian Ocean. From Asian societies, women are recruited separately for domestic labour. Since most of these states do not grant permanent resident status, the labour force rotates constantly. No permanent ethnocultural enclaves emerge. In the Persian Gulf region's Muslim societies, the exclusion of women – i.e. one half of the population – from education and wage labour outside the home exacerbates the need for foreign temporary workers. While booming centers such as Bahrain, Qatar, and the United Arab Emirates attract big companies and the wealthy, the high level of young people without job prospects creates an equally high potential for emigration and, seemingly, for fundamentalist movements, whose activities make admission into receiving societies more difficult for peaceful Muslim Arab migrants.

Sub-Saharan Africa is a seventh system of temporarily expanding economies, such as those of Somalia and Kenya and, since the end of apartheid, South Africa. However, dysfunctional elites (at first still colonizer-trained or colonizer-supported) created obstacles to development in some states, and equally disruptive World Bank-imposed cuts in social services exacerbated poverty and joblessness. Large-volume internal rural–urban moves and out-migration to former colonizer countries (which often refuse to grant admission papers) have been the consequence.

Finally, socialist East European countries were characterized by singular migration patterns. Since the right to work was guaranteed, labour migration to distant job-providing places was, seemingly, not necessary. However, collectivization, uneven rural–urban development, economic growth in Hungary and Yugoslavia and in sections of the USSR, and investments in southern Siberia did result in interregional and interstate mobility. Prohibition of emigration separated this macro-region from all other migration regions; admission of "Third World" students and workers under training programs did not usually result in diaspora formation. Since the collapse of the system in 1989, new East–West migrations have taken shape and centers such as Moscow or Prague attract internal, Chinese, and Western migrants.

At the turn to the twenty-first century, migrants across the world face the consequences of religious fundamentalisms, increasing xenophobia in many countries, and ever more stringent so-called homeland security barriers. On the other hand, many societies need migrants and many potential migrants need entryways to societies that permit sustainable lives. Economists' and social scientists' research based on data of the World Bank, the International Monetary Fund, and the United Nations Development Program indicate ever-growing disparities between the northern and southern hemispheres due to the imposition of tariff barriers and unequal terms of trade by the powerful North. Thus the potential for South–North migrations is being increased by the very policies of those countries reluctant to admit more migrants. Much of migration research in the last two decades has concentrated on these new patterns.

This chapter has summarized the history of migration – a central aspect of human lives and the creating of societies – because much of it has been rendered invisible by scholarship centered on nation-states and political events. Such writing considered in-migrating "foreigners" a "problem" to be studied, only to find remedies against such noxious elements detrimental to a body politic constructed as bordered and monocultural. Social and cultural history since the 1970s has indicated that societies have been many cultured throughout history and that national histories were an invention of nationalist-minded scholars from the mid-nineteenth to the mid-twentieth century.[30] Migration history and social sciences approaches to present-day migrations have entered a fruitful synthesis in the last two decades.

Bibliography

Appleyard, Reginald T., ed., *International Migration Today*, 2 vols. (Paris, 1988).

Cavaciocchi, Simonetta, ed., *Le migrazioni in Europa secc. XIII–XVIII* (Florence, 1994).

Cohen, Robin, ed., *The Cambridge Survey of World Migration* (Cambridge, 1995).

Dupeux, Georges, ed., *Les Migrations internationales de la fin du XVIIIe siècle à nos jours* (Paris, 1980).

Gungwu, Wang, ed., *Global History and Migrations* (Boulder, CO, 1997).

Hoerder, Dirk, Christiane Harzig, and Adrian Shubert, eds, *The Historical Practice of Diversity: Transcultural Interactions from the Early Modern Mediterranean to the Postcolonial World* (New York, 2003).

Kritz, Mary M., Lin L. Lim, and Hania Zlotnik, eds, *International Migration Systems: A Global Approach* (Oxford, 1992).

Marks, Shula, and Peter Richardson, eds, *International Labour Migration: Historical Perspectives* (London, 1984).

Pan, Lynn, gen. ed., *The Encyclopedia of the Chinese Overseas* (Richmond, Surrey, 1999).

Parnwell, Mike, *Population Movements and the Third World* (London, 1993).

Simon, Rita J., and Caroline B. Brettell, *International Migration: The Female Experience* (Totowa, NJ, 1986).

Skeldon, Ronald, *Population Mobility in Developing Countries: A Reinterpretation* (New York, 1990).

3
Theories of Migration and Cultural Interaction

This chapter provides, first, a critical assessment of approaches to and theories of migration history from the 1880s to the 1950s, including the neo-classical economics hypotheses. Concepts and terms such as push and pull factors need careful attention as regards their achievements as well as shortcomings. Clichés of uprooted migrants and of newcomers culturally in limbo, which are still part of public debates, need to be deconstructed. We will then discuss early innovative concepts, especially Latin American ones since the 1930s. Next we turn to typologies of migrations and to historiographical subfields restricted to one particular type. We pay attention to issues of race, including whiteness, and gender or, more particularly, the inclusion of women in migration history. In conclusion, we will discuss research paradigms developed since the 1970s, in particular comparative or global ones. Chapter 4 will then synthesize concepts of the present.

According to the literature accessible, little research was undertaken outside of Western Europe and North America. However, in politics, migration was high on the agenda in British India as regards contract labourers, in the imperial powers' relations with China, and in Japan as it expanded into Korea and Manchuria. Labour supply was an issue in all regions of fast economic development and in specific locations such as plantations or mines, where production was concentrated. Migration politics generated some expert opinions and data collection.

In the 1880s, when the growth of industry in the Atlantic World demanded massive in-migration of factory workers either from rural regions or from other states, social reformers and the emerging disciplines of sociology, political economy, and political science began to show interest in population mobility. Social reformers generally placed human beings, migrants or not, at the center of their interest; scholars dealt with institutions in the new disciplines, often called "state sciences" (*Staatswissenschaften* in German) rather than "social sciences." To migrant "Others" they often assigned traits of inferiority. Political economists dealt with migrant and resident workers as factors of production. Population planners wanted quantitative data for framing policies of encouraging or restricting in-migration or to get rid of "paupers" who were part of the nation but without job prospects. Most research was done in receiving societies and was often couched in terms of immigrants as social problems.

Local and regional historians in Western Europe, the US, and Canada usually have taken note of migration and the presence of people from elsewhere. Such meticulously detailed histories have been denigrated as full of "unimportant" matters. However, are migrants' lives unimportant? The local data and those concerning individuals are central to the writing of the history of common men and women, whether resident or migrant. For nineteenth-century historians concerned only with nations and top-level policy-making or politicking, "non-national" migrants were of no importance. Writing the story of a nation imposes a restraining frame – developments and human lives that begin and end elsewhere count little.

3.1   Theory and Practice from the 1880s to the 1950s

Sophisticated collection of empirical data on migration began in the contexts of (1) eighteenth-century urbanization and increasing mobility within European states, (2) the nineteenth-century transatlantic mass migrations, and (3) twentieth-century northern Chinese migrations to Manchuria. The division of industrial labour into ever simpler and more repetitive tasks initiated by US engineer Frederick W. Taylor (1856–1915) reduced the need for skilled workers and increased demand for "unskilled" and low-waged men and women. Similarly, mass production in plantations required deskilling of unfree African and Asian workers. Migration thus often involved a loss of skills acquired before departure and useful in the societies of origin, since they were unusable in the new post-migration jobs markets. The mass mobility was a major factor of economic growth but was viewed with unease by middle classes and political elites who benefited from the migrants. Middle-class observers lumped together poorly paid migrants and the resident poor as social "problems," potential criminals, or "the dangerous classes" unfit for (full) membership in the nation.

Migration is often studied as cross-border international movements. But, within Europe, migrations to industrializing centers and mining regions involved far larger numbers of migrants from adjacent rural areas or from afar than did the transatlantic moves. From the seventeenth and eighteenth centuries, mercantilist policies resulted in data collection about the numbers of resident local, absent emigrant, and in-migrant populations and their productive capacities. The increasing sophistication of data collection and of interpretation is particularly well studied for the Habsburg monarchy, self-defined as "state of many peoples." At the turn to the twentieth century, economist Leopold Caro perceptively argued that, although no emigration policy existed, the new and aggressive Austrian-German nationalism – like that of Europe's other imperial governments – indirectly forced people of different cultures and on the margins to emigrate through cultural discrimination and state investment, i.e. job creation, only in the national core regions.[1]

Mobilization of factory labour in Great Britain and decennial census data permitted social geographer Ernest G. Ravenstein to study internal rural-to-urban migrants. His unfortunate term "laws of migration" (1885) led subsequent scholars to neglect his work, since social phenomena may follow patterns but are not "laws." His understanding of English migrations applies to other European societies of the period: more migrants move over short distances than over larger ones; in the region of origin "vacancies" left by the out-migrants may be filled by in-migrants from more remote places; migrants select centers of commerce and industry with income-generating jobs as destinations; and women are more mobile than men.[2] Across Europe, ideology motivated interest in internal migrations: peasant families were considered the basis of a "healthy" society, while "shiftless" industrial workers were considered to have questionable lifeways and thought to be a political threat to the ruling classes.

To nation and class, race was added as a category in the debates in the late nineteenth century. Emigration of nationals caused concern if their productive capacity was lost to the state but was welcomed if population planners wanted to "shovel out" an assumedly unproductive "surplus" of mobile poor people, disabled war veterans, unmarried women, and orphaned children. In the imperial British "Empire Settlement" program, bureaucrats sent such "white" migrants to the "coloured" segments of the empire to improve or "whiten" them. In Germany, sociologist and political economist Max Weber understood the demand for East European, especially Polish, migrant workers but pronounced them to be racially inferior. The attitudes of respective nations' scholars to Italians in France, Czechs in Vienna, or East European Jews in many societies were similarly skewed. This "scientific" racism deeply affected migrants' chances of inserting themselves into receiving societies, since academic pronouncements and stateside migration policies were often linked.

Within Britain, reform-minded scholars would settle in a working-class or immigrant neighbourhood, underserviced by the municipality, to help people *and* study their lives at the same time (Toynbee Hall, London). This "settlement house" concept influenced data-based research in other countries. In the United States, deeply divided racially by the prior free and unfree migrations, highly educated middle-class women researched the "problems growing out of the social conditions" rather than label poor people as a "social problem." Like reformers in Canada, Edith Abbott, Sophonisba Breckinridge, Florence Kelley, and many others collected data. Jane Addams and the researcher-residents of Chicago's Hull House (founded 1889) understood that what were perceived as bordered, territorial "ethnic ghettos" were, in fact, mixed neighbourhoods in which migrants of many cultures mingled and created distinct social spaces.[3] The data on immigrants and on the poor in general were intended to inform legislators to pass reform legislation.

Social reform, Christian ethics, and the emerging discipline of sociology were one integrated field. Research was gendered. While the studies of women influence scholarship to the present as models of empirical research, university teachers, all men, debated immigrants' shortcomings and immigrant assimilation. At the University of Chicago's School of Sociology the men asked: Would migrants give up their old world ways? Could they be changed so as to cease to be the – assumed – threat to political and social structures? In the anglophone British-origin World, parliamentary commissions would pose such questions to experts and opinion leaders. In Canada, royal commissions inquired into the lives and presumed deficiencies of Italian and Asian immigrants. The US Senate's Immigration ("Dillingham") Commission published a 41-volume *Report* (1911–12). While the resulting important data collections became sources for later scholarship, the commissions' racializing interpretations, usually unsupported by their own data, have been discarded. In Great Britain, economic historian William Cunningham, avoiding the limitations of nationalist perspectives, studied migrants as producers and contributors to society. In *Alien Immigrants to England* (1897) he proposed a worldwide perspective and called for a "wise policy" to attract skilled immigrants. However, a parliamentary commission on "alien immigration" (1903) resulted in the (anti-)Aliens Act of 1905. Nation-state governments were unwilling to support their policies for economic growth with policies to attract and integrate immigrant workers.

Robert E. Park of the Chicago School of Sociology and his colleagues conceptualized "assimilation" as interpenetration and fusion by which individuals, groups, and societies would achieve a common culture. However, he took an absorptive power of established institutions for granted and saw ethnic groups or "races" as less developed and thus as to be incorporated according to the motto *e pluribus unum* – unity out of the many – into a society that was implicitly white and

Anglo (and male). Still, in the context of the times, Park was reform-minded and never submitted to the period's rabid white-supremacy ideology. As editor of the Carnegie Corporation's "Americanization" series he was influential far beyond his own research. "Assimilation," which is understood to imply a surrender of traits of the culture of origin to become part of the new majority society, has been replaced in research since the 1980s by concepts of acculturation, accommodation, insertion, and adjustment.[4]

Ethnologist William I. Thomas, an internal migrant from a small rural community via a southern university town to the metropolis of Chicago, felt that on his way he had traversed three centuries. With a cultural anthropology approach, he studied the life-histories of Polish migrants and, in distinction to many of his colleagues, acknowledged that without language capability no other culture may be studied. Jointly with Polish philosopher and sociologist Florian W. Znaniecki, he developed a concept of culturally embedded subjective meanings of empirical data. They advocated a "life-history" or biographical approach to immigrant culture that contextualizes men's and women's lives in the double bind of culture of origin and receiving culture. The continuity in migrants' lives was spelled out in *The Polish Peasant in Europe and America* (5 vols, 1918–20).

The community of reformer-scholars was transnational and transatlantic. German social scientist Georg Simmel's discussion of "The Stranger" as being in the community but not of it influenced Robert Park in the US.[5] William Thomas connected to Russian scholars, sociologist and theorist Pitirim Sorokin among them, and later to the Swedish sociologists Gunnar Myrdal and Alva Myrdal.[6] From among US scholars, Jane Addams visited England's social reformers; Florence Kelley studied at the University of Zurich, where Russian women who would struggle for social reform in the tsarist empire pursued their education; and Emily Greene Balch, who had studied with the French political economist and sociologist P. Émile Levasseur, published *Our Slavic Fellow-Citizens* (1910) when "scientific racism" singled out Slavs as inferior and when racist groups in the US struggled for their exclusion. In Canada, many reformers-sociologists-educators influenced by British or French research published "applied sociology" studies on immigrants in particular regions or cities.[7] From Russia, via Germany, France, and Britain, to the Americas, scholars in the newly emerging social sciences attempted to understand whole societies and migrants in them.

After the destructions of World War I, scholarly developments in the North Atlantic World diverged. From the nationalist historiography's racist classification of non-ethnic and migrant Others, it was only one more step to their assignment to forced migration and slave labour, to their deportation to marginal lands, or – worst – to extermination camps. In Germany, which had had to rely on foreign labour since the mid-1880s, demographer Friedrich Burgdörfer advocated deportation of non-German peoples.[8] In Great Britain, the arrival of East European Jewish refugees from pogroms and persecution in Russia had led to "research" confirming their inferiority. In France, equally in need of labour migrants, George Mauco, who in *Les Étrangers en France* (1932) posited that Frenchness implied natural superiority, became influential as population planner both under the fascist Vichy regime and in the French Republic of the 1950s. West European approaches to immigration, with few exceptions, were racist.

In contrast, in Poland, home to Poles, Jews, Germans, Bielo-Russians and Ukrainians, and with a long history of emigration, young multilingual anthropologists of the 1930s reflected the Central European academic migratory circuits. Trained at universities in Warsaw, Krakow, Vienna, Lwow/Lviv/Lemberg, Leipzig, Berlin, Paris, and, in some cases, London and the United States, and even in exile in Siberia, they were part of the humanist transcontinental and transatlantic community of migration scholars. W. I. Thomas had connected to this group. Krystyna Duda-Dziewierz focused on peasant villages in terms of both the development of national culture and the transnational aspects of migration: which strata left, what socialization they took with them, how the village society changed when migrants returned. Among Poles – as among Italians – mass emigration was multidirectional and diasporas emerged.[9]

In the 1920s and 1930s, international comparison resulted in a major statistical achievement, the two-volume

International Migrations (1929, 1931) of Walter F. Willcox and Imre Ferenczi, working for the non-partisan National Bureau of Economic Research (New York) and the International Labour Office's Migration Section (Geneva). They defined emigrants as all persons changing residence across state borders (including those between states and their colonies) intra- or intercontinentally, with the intention to reside abroad for over a year. The authors consolidated data from countries of departure, of transit, and of destination, and they emphasized that labour migration includes a consciousness of class and could be unfree: labour "emigrants" from Europe, "emigrants from Africa as slaves," and "semi-voluntary or indentured emigrants from Africa, Asia and Polynesia" needed to be dealt with on par. Their term "proletarian mass migration" has been used ever since. The transatlantic community of scholars could rely on a global community of statisticians.[10]

Research in Poland and data collection worldwide highlighted the massive problems involved in emphasis on nation-state-created data.

1   Poland, carved up in 1795 by the three neighbouring empires, and peoples without a territory, such as Jews or Roma ("Gypsies"), are left out of the data.
2   The "nationality" principle in statistics turns all departing or arriving persons from countries with many cultural groups into members of the hegemonic national culture.
3   Aggregate "emigration" perspective data do not reflect multidirectional departures. Similarly, immigration statistics, for example of "Chinese," do not reflect regional cultures and languages.

Such statistics incorporate migrants from particular cultures into the majority ethnocultural (or national) group, thus distorting cultural differences. Social and cultural history approaches to migration need to disaggregate the data if possible.

Outside of the Atlantic World, migration research was slow to develop – some scholars argue that colonizer rule retarded independent academic activity.[11] When, between the 1890s and 1937, tens of millions of northern Chinese migrated to Manchuria (after 1932 Japanese-controlled Manchukuo), the educated elite paid little attention to those considered "faceless ciphers." In contrast, the (Japanese-owned) South Manchuria Railway Company in the 1920s and 1930s hired social scientists for data collection, assessments of labour demand in Manchuria, and research on the conditions that pushed rural men and families out. The Nankai Institute of Economic Research in Tianjin, founded by economist He Lian (or Franklin Ho, PhD Yale), played a prominent role in the research. In distinction to US narratives about frontiers, migrants were not stylized as "pioneers" or "tough" but saw themselves as simple, hardworking people capable of enduring difficult conditions. In the People's Republic of China after 1949 interest in working-class and peasant migrants concentrated only on those who had struggled for the communist victory.[12]

While transcontinental historians and statisticians developed a global perspective to migrant insertion into economic sectors and data, and while social reformers chose a transnational humanist perspective to migrant lifeways and cultures, nation-state-confined historians pursued a narrow "nation-to-ethnic enclave" approach: migrants left a national territory (rather than a region or class) and ended up in an ethnic ghetto. Unable to cope with the culture and institutions in the new society, they clannishly stuck to the ways of their old world, self-segregating in Irish Cabbagetowns, Chinatowns, or Little Italies. The quintessential statement of this view was Oscar Handlin's study of Irish migrants in Boston, *The Uprooted* (1951). The title, which became a catchword and reverberated in Alex Haley's search for his African origins (*Roots*, 1976), did not reflect Handlin's recognition that "the great migrations made the American people" and that "immigrants were American history." Handlin wrote in the context of the intensive debate about admission of "displaced persons" from fascist Germany's forced labour camps and the ravages of war, people uprooted indeed. But even they made choices to reorient their lives.[13] Caroline Ware's *Greenwich Village* (1935), in contrast, provided a community study of continuities in first- and second-generation immigrant adaptation as well as of intergenerational cultural transfer and change. Ware placed herself in the humanist approach:

first, the conviction that the student of any human situation must bring to his study a fundamental and genuine respect for the people and institutions studied and a determination to view them first and foremost in their own terms; and, second, the assumption that all types of material, whatever their source and form, may shed light on a problem if they are regarded as evidence and are subjected to the tests and criticism which all evidence demands.[14]

3.2   Neo-Classical Economics and the Push–Pull Model

In public discussions as well as in scholarship a "push–pull" model has been applied to migrants' decision-making: less developed state economies push people out, those with higher wages and standards of living pull them in. This formula simplifies the complex, many-layered societies and intercultural settings: migrants may choose to depart in view of limited economic options and coercive social orders; they seek information on the complex societal insertion processes and labour market options in receiving societies.

Neo-classical economists, transforming the push–pull terminology into a reductionist cost–benefit analysis, have argued that rural areas or whole countries with low wages and a high supply of workers are unattractive to wage-earners. In comparison to cities or countries with high wages and growing industries, the wage differential would explain behaviour in an "immigration market." People – like goods – would be "traded" across interregional boundaries according to supply and demand. The resulting equalization of factor prices would reduce the differential and thus migration. These approaches emerged in the 1950s and 1960s in response to Western concern about the developing world and rural–urban migrations.[15] They were thought to predict migration "flows," adaptation patterns of migrants with specific economic characteristics, and their impact on the receiving country's economy.[16]

This income-centered model was criticized from within the field of economics because it neglects standard of living and prices for food and housing. Neo-classical economics focuses on production, for which quantifiable data exist, and neglect consumption expenses and family economies, since no data were recognized to exist in the 1960s. However, migrants, most of whom cannot afford to return, base their decisions on wage levels and costs of living as specific to their class. Under the classical gender division of tasks, they supplement (men's) wage incomes by (women's) judicious management of expenses, substitute home production for scarce monetary income, and add income by casual labour of family members. Even the neo-classical economists' focus, "male breadwinners," would have suggested the question: "What was the cost of bread?" In many cultures, labour migration was a generic "migration to bread." In late twentieth-century migrations of women as caregivers, domestics, or nursing professionals, gender roles may be reversed, but the income–expenditure comparison remains part of migrants' calculations.

Reacting to the critique, neo-classic economists refined the macro-approach to include the micro-level of decision-making but selected a rational choice approach in which potential and actual migrants view the cost of migration as an investment in their human capital and select their destination according to income-maximization criteria. While this approach to detailed calculating costs of migration did differentiate the vague stories of narrative historians, migrant men and women negotiated many rationalities rather than proceeding by mere income-maximization.

In the 1950s and 1960s scholarly rational choice advocates had to recognize that, in developing societies, rural–urban migration occurred even though agricultural pursuits continued to yield family-supporting income while high urban unemployment rates made jobs difficult to find or hold down. Economists responded by differentiated calculations of long-term expectations of migrants and estimated yields of the migration decisions. Such analyses replaced the "bright lights and many diversions" cliché of cityward mobility. But, again, reliance on rational choices – now in the plural – was undercut by including too few variables into analyses. People negotiate between risk diversification, family strategies, personal life-course expectations, emotional factors, oppressive (but non-quantifiable) conditions in the locality of origin, and intergenerational aspirations for the lives of (future) children.

Still, the economic approaches helped to jettison both the uprootedness and the retention-of-culture clichés. Given the methodological chasm, however, economists and social historians hardly cite each other's works.[17] (For recent developments in migration economics see chapter 3.5.)

3.3 Innovative Concepts of Transculturation, 1930s–1950s

At the height of the US melting pot ideology, epitomized in British intellectual Israel Zangwill's drama of that title,[18] and of Americanization policies, public intellectuals such as Randolph S. Bourne understood that "America is coming to be, not a nationality but a trans-nationality, a weaving back and forth, with the other lands, of many threads of all sizes and colors." No democratic society needs to "fly into panic at the first sign" of migrants' self-determination and cultural expressions, and, according to Horace Kallen's conceptualization of "cultural pluralism," states are federations of nationalities rather than monocultural nations.[19] However, racist views as expressed in Madison Grant's *The Passing of the Great Race* (1916) proved stronger: the US government imposed exclusion measures on migrants from Europe in 1917.

Outside the core of the white Atlantic, in Brazil and Cuba as well as in Canada, sophisticated theorizations emerged after 1930. In Brazil, sociologist Gilberto Freyre, influenced by Columbia University's anthropologist Franz Boas, argued that the mixing (*mestiçagem*) of migrants from Europe and Africa with Native Peoples, in a process of ethnogenesis, established a new, culturally richer people. Population planners and advocates of "race hygiene," in contrast, decried the "mongrelization" of assumedly pure races and demanded policies to attract European migrants to "whiten" Latin American societies. Freyre's view, that within power relations the lives of the Afro-Brazilian slaves and Portuguese–Brazilian masters were inextricably linked, has since been widely criticized as too positive a view of the colonizers' capability to establish harmonious and paternalist multiracial societies. Still, his concept of a frontier society built by both the powerless and the powerful immigrants was a major theoretical innovation. For Argentina, Gino Germani, in *Estructura social de la Argentina* (1955), discussed acculturation of immigrants from Europe as well as internal migration from rural to urban zones during the period of industrialization.[20]

In Cuba's many-cultured society, Fernando Ortiz, in 1940, developed the concept of transculturation in the economic, institutional, legal, ethical, religious, artistic, linguistic, psychological, sexual, and other aspects of people's lives. He differentiated the cultures of Native Peoples, Iberians and other Europeans, and Africans into their components – Wolof, Catalonian, Genoese, Jewish, Ciboney, Cantonese – to arrive at an empirically sound concept of fusion in power hierarchies. Like Freyre, he saw the Iberian peninsula as a bridge between Europe and Africa, as a space where cultures interacted.[21] The concept of transculturation, also explored by Bronisław Malinowski,[22] emphasizes the creation of cultures that include aspects of all their contributors' pre-migration practices but are different and new. Similar but more gendered approaches were later used to understand the Native–French and Native–Scottish *métissage* in eighteenth- and nineteenth-century Canada's fur trade as well as the intermingled Portuguese–African and –Asian families in the Indian Ocean trading enclaves.[23]

Freyre's and Ortiz's studies, available in English by 1946 and 1947, did not become part of North Atlantic scholarship until re-read in the 1970s. In Canada, at bicultural McGill University in Montreal, Everett Hughes and Helen McGill Hughes, both trained at the University of Chicago, argued that receiving societies provide no single model of acculturation.[24] All of these empirically based analyses and theorizations challenged the ideology of nation-state homogeneity but, in their time, could not prevail against master narratives.

In a further distinct development of the 1920s and 1930s, students and other intellectual migrants from the French colonies to France and from India to Great Britain conceptualized intercultural fusion and resistance in terms of colonizer power, migrations between metropoles and colonies, interactions, and colonized subalterns' strategies of subversion. In 1930s Paris, Léopold Senghor from Senegal and Aimé Césaire from Martinique tried to dissolve white–black antagonism through the concept of *négritude* – which uses the French language to celebrate African culture, turning the racial epithet "nègre" into a positive term in the process. Both were influenced by the African-Caribbean and African-American cultural protest in Harlem, with its ramifications in Paris through the network of black writers of Paulette Nardal, also from Martinique.[25] Alioune Diop, in his influential journal *Présence Africaine* (since 1947), asserted the value of the African expression in a dialogue with French ethnologists and intellectuals at a time when the first generation of West African labour migrants were being recruited for French industry. In Great Britain, the same role was taken by students from India. When, later, white scholars re-read the travel accounts of early Dutch and Portuguese traders in West Africa or of Jesuits in China, they realized that these travellers had been deeply impressed by the sophistication of these societies and their level of scholarly learning. The primitive–civilized dichotomy was an invention of nineteenth-century nationalist historians and ethnologists. The 1930s and 1940s dual migrations of workers and intellectuals reverberated back through remittances and return migration and challenged Europeans' cultural ascriptions. The critical analysis of Europe's self-proclaimed superiority by migrating intellectuals would impact movements for independence and post-colonial migrations.[26]

3.4 Towards a Typology of Migrations in Modern Times[27]

Since the 1990s, a comprehensive historiography of migrations analyzes migrants' decisions and trajectories in a spectrum from free to forced, the geographic space traversed from local to intercontinental, and the intended duration of migration from seasonal to lifetime. A typology of migrations – that needs gendering in each empirical application – would thus include

- free migrants who decide when to depart and where to go according to their own desires and life-projects within the frames states impose on out- and in-migration
- labour migrants, the traditional "free" migrants of the proletarian mass migrations and of the present South–North migrations, who decide to depart under often severe economic constraints
- bound labour migrants who have to sell their labour for a number of years because of poverty (European and Asian indentured servants)
- forced labour migrants who are enslaved for menial work for life (African slaves in the Atlantic World), enslaved for service or intellectual labour (Africans in the Indian Ocean World and people elsewhere), bound for a certain period of their life against their will (South Africa under apartheid), or kidnapped and placed in labour camps for an indeterminate period (Nazi Germany, imperial Japan, the Stalinist Soviet Union)
- involuntary migrants displaced by political intolerance (exiles), religious intolerance (religious refugees), or other causes, such as ethnic or gender-based inequalities
- refugees from war and other violence
- persons displaced by ecological disasters, whether natural or men[*sic*]-made.

Decision-making about departure, destination, and length of stay is best conceptualized in a continuum from relatively free, via different forms of constraints and coercion, to forced. Transatlantic and transpacific migrants of the nineteenth century and the Third World to First World migrants of the turn to the twenty-first century made and make decisions "free," albeit *under the constraints of economic conditions* that did and do not permit life-projects or even survival "at home." Women's decisions are further constrained by gendered roles and restrictions. Children generally have to follow their parents, even though they may resent being separated from friends and other family. Thus, people make "free" decisions within frames of reference at best and massive constraints at worst. Involuntary migrants, refugees, and exiles depart under political, ethno-racial, gender, or other persecution, or because of warfare within or between states, social

ostracism, fundamentalist religious pressures, and/or tradi-
tion-bound stagnation. Usually, refugees hope to return if
conditions improve in their society of birth. Forced migrants
are torn out of their social environments by military, police,
or private entrepreneurs, whether raiders for forced labourers, slave catchers, or traffickers in the sex trade.

Distance of migration may be short, medium, or long.
Long-distance migration may lead into similar occupations
and cultural environments. Indian Ocean port cities were part
of transoceanic commercial and migration networks with
similar labour practices and trading protocols. Young men,
who headed for work on another continent, often remained
in earth work – digging and shovelling on infrastructural
projects – and lived in a community of migrant compatriots.
On the other hand, geographic proximity does not necessarily
signify cultural proximity. Young women who move from
rural regions somewhere on the globe to domestic labour in
nearby towns and cities face the transition from peasant or
small-town life to a life with urban middle-class employers.
In the past, greater distance often involved higher travel cost
in terms of both transportation and time. Cost, however, also
depends on means of transport; land-bound voyaging is
usually more expensive than water-borne ship travel. Patterns
of migration and adjustment became time-compressed in the
mid-1870s with the introduction of steamships, and again in
the mid-1950s with air travel.

As regards intended duration, migration might be seasonal,
annual, multi-annual, for the duration of a working life, or
permanent. Across the globe, men and women, sometimes
with their children, have migrated and continue to migrate
seasonally to harvest work or to food processing or temporarily to mines or oil rigs. Multi-annual migrations might involve
moves to a distant branch of an internationally active
company, whether one of the eighteenth-century East India
companies or a late twentieth-century computer giant, or to
work as caregivers for infants, children, or the elderly in societies with a shortage of service workers. People might leave for
a number of years to gain additional experience in a craft or at
a university, to set up a branch of a family business, or for
income-generating reasons. Potential migrants often plan to
stay only for a number of years, but both poor labour markets

"at home" and adjustment to the receiving society may induce them to extend their sojourn. Some, wanting to return, become "unwillingly permanent" migrants because conditions in the society of origin remain uninviting, while others adjust and stay as "unintentionally permanent" migrants.

3.5 Compartmentalization of Research by Type of Migration

Under the division of historiography and the social sciences into ever more subfields, different types of migration have been slotted into different compartments of scholarship and have been approached with varying analytical concepts and methods. Transatlantic-minded scholars concerned themselves with "free" migrations, the history of transatlantic slavery remained a different field, Asian contract labourers formed yet another subfield, and refugees were segregated into a further slot. Internal migrants were dealt with separately from international ones – even though they often were the same persons. Ascriptions implied in terminologies and usages in public discourses produced further barriers: "free" migrants – a term that implicitly refers to Europeans – have the capability for political self-determination; slaves – implicitly Africans – lack initiative and intelligence; "coolies" – implicitly Asians – lead depraved lives. The imagery, rather than being related to regimes of bondage and forced migration, is projected back onto cultures of origin and colours of skin: inferior African societies, primitive "Indio" ones, or coolie-generating Asian ones. The complexity of naming is evident in the word "coolie" for self-indentured or kidnapped Asian labourers: white capitalists and workers used the term to signify cheap and despised men (and women). For Chinese labourers, "coolie" meant "bitter strength," for Tamils it indicated "wage for menial work," and in Gujarati ascription it signified members of the Kuli tribe. Making "coolie" the generic term of Indian Ocean labour migrants hid the fact that the vast majority of migrants moved without indenturing themselves. Scholars need to construct terminologies carefully and sensitively so as not to hurt those whose lives they investigate.

We select three types of migrants to discuss the separate research agendas in the historiography: Afro-Atlantic slaves, Asian contract labourers, and refugees. (Until the 1820s, we also need to remind ourselves, one-half to two-thirds of the European migrants arrived in the Americas under contracts of indenture.)[28]

African slave and free migrants' cultures had inspired Freyre's and Ortiz's theorizations of interaction in the plantation societies of the Americas from Brazil via Belize to the US South. In contrast, in the US, ascription of racial inferiority was abandoned only under the impact of the 1960s struggle for civil rights. Kenneth M. Stampp (1956) exposed the disastrous consequences of scholars' acceptance of the euphemism "peculiar institution" for the slave system, and Stanley Elkins (1959) asked how the institution of slavery – rather than their African origin – warped the lives and minds of the enslaved men, women, and children. With the blindfold of racism removed, scholars began to compare the slave societies of the Americas and quantify the forced migrations. Some 12 million were deported and, if they survived the Middle Passage, were part of the people that constructed the post-contact societies of the Americas. As regards the African side of the trade, investing human beings with agency implies assigning responsibilities. Coastal male-dominated warrior states supplied the slaves to European traders.[29] Comparative approaches analyze the chattel slave systems and slaves' lives in the US South, the Caribbean, and Brazil.[30] Other studies deal with slave migrations within Africa and in the Indian Ocean World – a region for which figures remain contested.[31] By the 1970s, scholarship turned to the impact of the African diaspora in the Atlantic World. But it took a publication as late as 1993, *The Black Atlantic*, to establish the theme in broader, even public debate.[32]

While scholarship in Africa and Asia could develop independently from colonizer control only with difficulty, the World of the Pacific was even further from the minds of scholars in the academe of "the West." The British imperial school of history had studied the Indian Ocean trade and the societies; from the early 1900s Anglo-North American perspective, Asia had appeared merely as a market rather than as a locus of cultures worth study. Early impulses came from Australia – the study of Chinese bound labourers in the

British Empire by Persia C. Campbell – and from the research by the Chinese scholar Ta Chen (Da Ch'en) on the impact of Chinese migrants in Southeast Asia and their communities of origin.[33] In the 1950s, empirical research was hampered: China had become communist in 1949 and, in the US, the Institute of Pacific Relations – a private non-partisan forum for the promotion of mutual understanding among nations of the Pacific Rim – succumbed to congressional Cold War investigations. After studies published mainly in Great Britain and independent India from the 1940s to the 1960s,[34] and a broadening of the field to include free and bound migration to the Philippines, Fiji, and Malaysia,[35] Hugh Tinker's massive survey of 1974 set the tone for analysis of the "second slavery."[36] Since then research has proliferated. Jan Breman and Valentine Daniel sensitively analyzed the experiences and identities of "coolies" as well as of the process of decultura-tion from regional affiliation to generic bound worker. Under indenture, some scholars argue, caste, class, and custom lost validity, and, once free from their indentures, men and women could avoid sliding back into such constraints. The most comprehensive survey is David Northrup's *Indentured Labor in the Age of Imperialism.*[37]

The migrations of African slaves, Asian contract labourers, European indentured servants, and Europeans departing under economic constraints often targeted separate destina-tions in the global system of labour importation by planta-tion, mine, and factory owners. In the Caribbean and in Hawai'i, however, planters experimented with labour from several origins when abolition of slavery became imminent after 1800. They ordered "trial shipments" of Asian workers, delayed abolition, had the British Parliament insert a semi-bound apprenticeship period after slavery, encouraged migra-tion of European workers, and discussed both male–female ratios and the desirability of single male vs. family labour migration. In the labour-importing societies, independent "passenger" migrants from India could speak with a voice of their own but this did not become part of Western migration historiography.[38] From the 1970s on, regionally specific research captured the migrant interactions and capitalist migrant worker relationships.[39] Recent research on planta-tion societies in the Americas and across the globe analyzes how slaves and slave owners, as forced and voluntary migrants, built societies.[40] The Worlds the slaves and the contract labourers made and the Worlds in which the plantation and mine owners lived were braided.

Like slaves and other bound working men and women, refugees arrive unprepared, have little negotiating power, and have to enter labour markets under disadvantageous conditions to rebuild their lives. In Europe and the Eastern Mediterranean, the convulsive change from multi-ethnic imperial to monocultural national states involved an "un-mixing" of peoples and massive refugee generation during and after the two world wars. After 1945, the moral revulsion at the Holocaust (Shoah) and Holocaust studies relegated refugee studies for several decades to a niche.[41] Retrospective works dealt with religious refugees in the Christian World since the sixteenth century[42] and with the Muslim and Christian Orthodox separation of peoples in the post-Ottoman regions. The deportation and near-genocide of the Armenians and the displacement of Kurdish people, neither of whom were granted a state of their own in 1918, has received attention only since the 1970s.[43] After World War II, the US, Canada, and Australia recruited many of Europe's displaced persons for labour under precarious conditions, but no comprehensive studies exist for Japan's refugee generation during the war in China and other parts of Asia.[44] Refugee generation in the decolonized World is analyzed by refugee studies centers, for example in Britain and Canada. German-language scholars as well as Aristide Zolberg and cooperating scholars have provided tentative synopses. The United Nations High Commissioner for Refugees publishes data collections and policy recommendations, and since 1980 the private US Committee for Refugees has issued the annual *World Refugee Survey.*[45]

3.6 New Approaches since the 1970s: World Systems, Family Economics, and Labour Markets

A comprehensive migration theory has not emerged in view of the many types of migrations, the compartmentalization of research by region, migrants' colour of skin and status, and the variety of societal structures. Both the late nineteenth-century "immigration to America" trope and the 1950s emphasis on a seemingly unitary developing world have sub-sided. Julius Isaac's theorization of "free" migrations (1947) did not overcome economic liberalism's basic contradiction: the self-regulating power of markets is not applied to labour markets, and state regulation of migration between labour markets is taken to be self-evident. Both Everett Lee and John Archer Jackson, in the 1960s, generalized from comparative data without a comprehensive frame of interpretation. Brinley Thomas's *Migration and Economic Growth* contains a good summary of the literature but no general theory.[46] By the end of the 1970s, first anthologies covering migrations in many parts of the world and employing a variety of methods and theories appeared.[47] But even at the end of 1990s, Jan Lucas-sen and Leo Lucassen cautiously entitled their anthology of recent approaches *New Perspectives* rather than "theory."[48]

From the 1970s, new theoretical and methodological approaches emerged. World systems theory centered on Latin America derived its interpretations from dependency theory, i.e. the analysis of Latin American economies as dependent on more powerful economic actors in the northern hemi-sphere. The new economics and the theory of segmented labour markets attempted to improve on neo-classical eco-nomic approaches. Emphasis on human agency and network approaches, including the study of social and individual human capital, focused on decision-making and experiences. Finally, concepts of transnationalism, transculturalism, and transregionalism began to be debated intensively.

The macro-level: world systems theory

In 1974, Immanuel Wallerstein's *The Modern World System* set off a debate about global economic development and migration. World systems theorists argue that, from the six-teenth century, world markets expanded from powerful capi-talist "core" countries through a "semi-periphery" to the "periphery." Regional disparities of location of raw materials such as minerals, and of the cost of their extraction, of plantation agriculture, and of industrial crops, led to inter-peripheral migrations. By the late nineteenth century, capital-ized and mechanized agriculture became more cost-effective than farms relying on human labour. Smallholding farm families were thus transformed into "surplus" labour, forced by economic circumstances to migrate to regions with income opportunities. This synthesis had been preceded by an analy-sis of the disparities between the post-1826 independent Latin American and Caribbean societies and the North Atlantic former colonizer World (André Gunder Frank and others) and by exchanges between economists in the African decolo-nizing World and those of the capitalist, ex-colonizer core. The resulting "dependency theory" dealt with unequal terms of trade, underdevelopment, and power relationships. Fernand Braudel studied dependencies and interdependencies in the Mediterranean from common people's lives in larger economic contexts. Janet Abu-Lughod, critiquing the Euro- and North Atlanto-centric perspective, differentiated world systems theory by emphasizing distinct thirteenth- and fourteenth-century trading circuits in the Asian–African–European World.[49] For the late twentieth century, Saskia Sassen emphasizes the connectedness of metropoles as centers of finance and of exploited migrant labour.

In world systems theory, migration is induced by the pene-tration of capitalist markets and production into peripheral societies. Investments dislocate local populations, and internal and international mobility reflect the flow of capital and goods but counter its direction. For cultural reasons (lan-guage, education, communication, transportation links), migration is directed from ex-colonies to former colonizer countries. Attempts by the states of destination to curtail the volume of migration are undermined by the policies of the World Bank and the International Monetary Fund which reduce social security for the populations in the migrant sending states. Where there have been threats to the invest-ments and profits of multinational companies, governments of the capitalist World have intervened militarily but in the process have generated large-scale internal and, often, cross-border refugee migrations – the Congo after independence, Guatemala, and Persia/Iran are examples. Scholars' analyses of these connections have not influenced political decisions.

The unequal terms of trade, set in the late twentieth and early twenty-first century by powerful economies with the support of the respective states, create the constraining conditions on peripheries that induce or force people to migrate. Economic disparities, hierarchies, and natural endowments influence conscious decisions of families and individuals to attempt to improve their material life. World systems perspectives provide a frame for a global approach to the economics of migration.

The micro-level: family economies

Micro-approaches, especially the concept of (family) economies in local economic and normative contexts, emerged from women's studies, family history, and gender studies and permitted the inclusion of non-measurable emotional and spiritual factors into the analysis of life-projects and migration decisions. Family economies, whether in peasant, industrial wage, or consumer societies, combine the income-generating capabilities of all family members with the family's income-allocation strategies to cover its reproductive needs, i.e. physical and emotional care for dependent children or elderly, and its consumption patterns. The pool of labour and emotional "quality" time is thus allocated according to societal norms to achieve the best possible results internally for the members of the family and, externally, for their standing in the community. Allocation of resources and duties has to be negotiated in terms of benefits for each: maximization of income or of leisure, child-care or out-work, education or wage-work for children, networking or individualist separation from the community. The process is neither equal nor democratic but depends on a person's stage in the family cycle and on their individual life-course; it also depends on traditional gender and generational hierarchies and on power relationships. More bluntly, in most societies family economies privilege older males over the rest of the family and male children over female children. The consensus aspect of the family-economy approach thus needs to be modified by a study of gender and intergenerational hierarchies. Furthermore, recent research has emphasized individual women's agency over family context.[50]

The "*new economics of labour migration*" began to study families' income-generating strategies at the same time independently – an indication of non-communication between scholarly disciplines. In distinction to the neo-classical economic approach, the new economists supported historians' empirical findings concerning out-migration from the rural regions of Europe or China. In agrarian and urban family strategies, migration decisions are made within kin or inter-related groups with the intent to increase revenues and minimize risks. Departure from the region of origin, which should not impact negatively on family status, is considered necessary to rectify shortcomings of statewide economic developments and market failure. Generating household income involves allocation of productive resources, diversification of sources of income among them, to guard against problems with any particular one. Diversification includes seasonal labour migration, sending specific family members to medium-distance jobs, or sending one family member to a long-distance location in the expectation that remittances will add to the household income.[51] Geographic diversification, i.e. economic and labour market diversification, supplements gendered diversification of tasks. Historically the restructuring of the textile sector from production in families to factory mass production led to the collapse of household economies in traditional producing regions. In the present, rural families in "developed" societies may rely on stateside crop insurance programs during crises in world markets or of climatic conditions. In "less developed" countries such support is usually not available or is prohibited by directives of the world's financial institutions dominated by the capitalist countries. Proactive migration patterns may establish security through alternative incomes. If no protective strategies or programs are available, disruptive developments force people into reactive mobility.[52]

The meso-level: labour market theory

The theory of labour market stratification and segmentation by Michael Piore and others revised the neo-classical economist assumption of one single pool of reserve labour and dovetailed with historians' empirical but less systematic findings. The concept of a dual labour market posits that state economies consist of a growing, capital-intensive, and often highly concentrated primary sector, in which jobs offer good pay and working conditions, employment stability, and opportunities for promotion. These are mostly reserved for native-born workers. A competitive, stagnating secondary sector provides irregular employment, low pay, and unpleasant or dangerous working conditions. European labour migrants in the US, in life-writings, described such insecurity and exploitation. The theory was amended to include a tertiary, marginal, or ghetto economy, which provides an even more insecure labour market. It forces workers to be highly flexible, a human resource that permits multiple responses during recessions. Furthermore, a critical assessment of the primary sector indicated problems with technological innovation or cyclical downswings. Around 1900, the US steel industry offered only irregular employment because of frequent breakdown of machinery, and around 2000 the electronics industry experienced booms, busts, and relocations.

Beyond the three-layered hierarchy, labour markets are segmented, segregated and stratified. Segmentation of labour markets follows tasks and skills; segregation prevents groups defined by gender or race or recent arrival from gaining access to better jobs; stratification involves horizontal barriers to advancement because of linguistic or technical knowledge, of age thresholds (seniority), or of other mechanisms. Migration and acculturation studies both indicate that temporary acceptance of unpleasant working conditions or wage levels offers entry-gates to job markets (and states) otherwise closed and show how irregular employment may fit men's and women's pre-migration experiences and child-care strategies. Empirical data demonstrate that, for migrants, job access is of primary concern. Thus, after the beginning of a recession, migrant arrivals decline even when wages and wage differentials stay at the same levels.[53]

Richard Edwards, Michael Reich, and David Gordon noted that rural–urban moves and interstate mobility were facilitated by the late nineteenth-century homogenization and internationalization of industrial labour markets. This homogenization involved processes of deskilling and occurred earlier in commercialized agriculture (latifundia, plantations) and in mining. In skilled occupations frequency of migration was lower, but German artisans, English and Scottish engineers, Welsh miners, and men and women of other cultures in particular trades could enter labour markets across many societies.[54]

Analyses of labour market segmentation emphasize that migrants do not compete for jobs with native-born working men and women but enter only segments commensurate with their skills or lack of them. Beyond labour market characteristics, other contexts impacted migrant insertion. Migrants may arrive with skills unusable in the receiving societies. Some research assumes that migrants from rural economies or less developed societies need to be socialized into regular work habits of assembly-line production. However, machinery inefficiency and fluctuating markets – historically in the Atlantic World's industrializing regions, in the present in Mexico's *maquiladora* industries or the Philippines' "export processing zones" – may deregularize a previous flexible habitus developed in home or rural economies in which one task may always be substituted for another.[55] In countries which, since the mid-1960s, introduced rigorous selection regimes for in-migration (points systems, rotational recruitment, admission for specific sectors of the labour market only), market forces and policies interact beyond what labour market theory may explain.

3.7 Recent Approaches: Agency, Networks, and Human and Social Capital[56]

According to their own life-writings and oral accounts, migrants, when making decisions about their lives in the context of family, community, and local–regional options, want to take responsibility for a share of family income-generation or to be "independent." They may also want to free themselves from constraining norms and traditional patterns of life. At the same time, they accept that they will have to adjust to the norms and patterns of the society of destination. Sociologist Anthony Giddens proposes to view structures as both the frame for agency and the outcome of social action (structuration theory). We call these *"processual structures"* and *"structured processes,"* concepts that emphasize dynamism, change, and interaction between individuals or social groups and context. Structures undergo constant if often slow change. They are not permanent. Processes in turn are not chaotic; they follow patterns. Migrants leave and enter evolving societal and state structures and, in the process, change societies of origin and arrival.[57] Such agency, rather than being voluntarist, is embedded in social *habitus* (Bourdieu), a system of dispositions and practices: people internalize norms and by their practices under changing circumstances develop or challenge them. Migration research as (historical) anthropology is concerned with the "spaces of agency" created by mobile people within existing-evolving structures.[58]

The scope of agency is dependent on the *"human capital"* or personal resources and on the "social capital" or networks a person has been encouraged to develop in the process of socialization and has augmented in adolescent and adult life. "Resources" refer to a person's pool of capabilities, and "capital" suggests a desire to invest such capabilities in achieving goals and life-course projects. Human capital includes social skills, professional expertise, languages, capability for emotional coping, and strategic competences. Such resources or funds of knowledge are of particular importance in the process of departure from a known and experienced community and insertion into a differently structured destination with unfamiliar patterns of social habitus. Among them are the competence to adjust expectations and strategies to unexpected "social environments" at destination and to engage in "negotiating" different goals, obstacles, and routes.

"Social capital" denotes people's ability to mobilize resources, to use structures and institutions, and to form supportive associations. To negotiate between multiple demands and options requires capabilities to select within community contexts, to mobilize resources from supportive networks of kin, friends, and acquaintances, and to express one's own cultural identifications and interests without alienating the supportive network. Social capital may serve as resource, as goal-orientation, but also as social control. The processes of social capital accumulation influence issues of belonging and

adaptation, inclusion and exclusion, crises and violence, security and economic development, both on the individual and on the societal level. Exclusion of particular groups from accumulation of social capital, such as lack of educational institutions for migrant youth, poses challenges not only to the disadvantaged individuals but also to the respective society's cohesion. Access to – or exclusion from – social capital and its activation by individuals influences social transformations.[59]

Migrants and non-migrants pursue their goals and projects in the context of other human beings, the immediate family, the community, and society as a whole – in *networks* of relations. These may operate in neighbourhoods, ethnocultural communities, workplace, faith-based congregations, age-centered peer groups, or other places. For migrants, networks are the connections to both the community of origins and the new community. Networks help to bridge distances, to collect information in order to gauge consequences of intended mobility, to adapt to larger state-mandated frames, to pass entry regimes, and to negotiate acculturation regulations. Networks may undercut the institutional side of migration regulation, though they usually do not operate against institutions. The practice of sequential ("chain") migration is based on networks: previous migrants send back information – their knowledge and the "prepaid tickets" they send are the social capital of "migrants-in-waiting," whose arrival with human capital then increases the social capital of the earlier arrived ones. In the early twentieth century, 94 percent of all migrants arriving in the US went to family and friends. Globally, this has been studied for diasporas of Chinese, Polish, Lebanese, and Italians. Migrant networks influence continuity and expansion but also contraction or shifting of particular migrant "flows." In addition they permit decisions based on cultural and emotional affinity. They allow employers to send trusted employees back to the home region to recruit additional personnel and they let inexperienced migrants find help at the destination. Networks, from the outside, seem amorphous, since they function according to an invisible, internal logic. Thus they cannot easily be controlled or managed by receiving societies, which intend to structure, frame, or limit migration.[60]

With their funds of knowledge and their capabilities, migrants move internally across administrative or internationally across state borders. Data on mobility are often collected at such borders and, thus, migration historians have paid great attention to them. Political boundaries, however, have little meaning for socio-geographic trajectories of migrants who pursue their own *mental maps*, which reflect networks, aspirations, and goals. Such mental-social maps are structured by the local starting point and role of kin and friends across the globe. Late nineteenth-century Italian migrants could talk about parents, siblings, cousins as if they all lived in close proximity when, in fact, they might live in Buenos Aires, Montreal, and Milan. Depending on projects, migrants might view Italy as "at home" or "back in Italy." Henri Lefèbvre conceptualized such meanings of places by differentiating geographic place into perceived, conceived, and lived space. The first refers to places as they are viewed by people in their particular mental frames, the second to projects of transforming nature in order to serve a particular individual's needs, the third to the way people live in particular locations. Such triply layered mental maps include a time line from past to future. They concern regions in which income-generating activities are possible and routes through which remittances may be sent to family in the place of birth. Mental maps, like networks, are flexible and changing. Since they are informal, it is difficult for migration scholars to understand or reconstruct them.[61]

Two concepts attempt to capture such mental, non-state geographies: *"diaspora"* and *"scape."* "Diaspora," used originally for the Jewish and the Hellenistic or Greek dispersal and cultural interaction, refers to communities in many societies (within different political territories) that are linked to one another and to the place of origin. They are socially interdependent but spatially dispersed. Such communities share – or believe they share – a common culture. Analytically, the "common culture" may be a construction; empirically it varies between the several societal structures in which the diasporic communities live. The everyday practices of, for example, diasporic Chinese vary between Australia, France, Sweden, Canada, and South Africa. Diasporas connect non-contiguous cultural groups through real or imagined bonds across macro-regional, hemispheric, or global spaces.[62]

To theorize migrants' location of origin and of actual living, Homi Bhabha has coined the term "third space." In the process of acculturation, migrants neither duplicate the culture of origin nor merge into the culture of arrival; rather they create a fusion, a new, third place or space. In a more flexible way, Arjun Appadurai suggests avoiding designations that refer merely to physical or political geography ("place") and expanding the notion of social "spaces" to a social space filled with meanings, "*scapes.*" Continents, Africa or Europe for example, suggest "a particular configuration of apparent stabilities for permanent associations between space, territory, and cultural organization" that has, in fact, been constructed only recently from particular viewpoints and from particular interests. Traditional cartography of large landmasses has equated immovable geographic continents with changing societies. In contrast, "space" is the sum of physical environment and stateside and societal institutions, as created and changed in everyday practices and interpersonal relations. Usage of spaces creates "*scapes*" – family-scapes, ethnocultural scapes, mediascapes, and others. While "diaspora" refers to a group and its origin, "scape" refers to people and their multiple contexts in the present, including an orientation towards options in the future – not merely an expectation of one single path of life. "Scapes" are flexible, have shifting, permeable, or gliding boundaries, are perspectival from the point of view of particular human beings or groups, and may incorporate multiple attachments and consumer preferences.[63]

Spaces and scapes overlap and interact. Students migrating from countries of the worldwide Francophonie to France in Europe live in a particular, usually underserviced, *banlieue*. They are part of ethnocultural scapes sometimes imposed on them by their elders or ascribed by French public discourse; they may feel at home in a music-scape that extends to Caribbean–Latin American productions mediated through globalized companies such as the Japanese-origin Sony; they are in a techno-scape through which they communicate globally. To understand modern migrants' places–regions–spaces, Allen F. Roberts has applied the concept of "space" and "process" to particular migrant groups' views of their "territories." Such "processual geographies" combine continent of origin as an ecumene with multiple ethnoscapes and smaller transnationalisms that translate into a network of spaces. An example is a small group, the Mourides, from the island of Mauritius in the Indian Ocean, originating in Asia, following a Senegalese Islamic sufi belief system, and living in places as distant as Los Angeles. The concept of "scapes" permits a flexible understanding of migrant communities, families, and individuals in their several local, regional, statewide, and global extensions.[64]

3.8 Transnational Approaches and Transcultural Societal Studies

In contrast, a macro-level conceptualization of migrations at the turn to the twenty-first century was the reintroduction, in the early 1990s, by US anthropologists and sociologists studying Latin American migrants of the concept of "*transnationalism*." Nina Glick Schiller, Linda Basch, and Cristina Blanc-Szanton's influential *Towards a Transnational Perspective on Migration* and subsequent publications by Alejandro Portes and his colleagues gave the term wide currency in the migration and globalization discourses, both scholarly and public. In a critique of the presentism of the approach, Nancy Foner noted that "transnationalism has been with us for a long time, and a comparison with the past allows us to assess just what is new about the patterns and processes involved in transnational ties today." Kiran Patel discussed usages of the term since Bourne had introduced it in 1916 (see chapter 3.3 above), and Peter Kivisto added a critical evaluation.[65] Given the continuing importance of nation-states in regulating migration, the concept does provide a perspective on developments since the rigidification of borders in the last decades of the nineteenth century. *Trans*national does not refer to distinct entities that engage in negotiations (*inter*national relations) or whose distinct legal regulations for business systems have to be taken into account (*inter*national trade, *multi*national companies). It refers to continuities in migrants' experiences: the simultaneous living of aspects of different cultures, the intersocietal and transfamilial economic nexus of remittances, the emotional ties between family members in two or more cultural spaces. "People, ideas, and institutions do not have clear national identities. Rather, people may translate and assemble pieces from different cultures. Instead of assuming that something was distinctively American [or German, Chinese, Brazilian, Kenyan, . . .], we might assume that elements of it began or ended somewhere else."[66]

Transnational approaches, however, continue to rely on territories as basic units, criticized by Appadurai and others. Critics of the concept of nation emphasize that such constructed units are no longer identity-providing communities of fate.[67] Saskia Sassen and others point to the importance of the world's metropoles, and historians of migration have emphasized regional belongings. Migrants from Lancaster left with different identities and experience than those from Sussex, and migrants from Luzon, Philippines, leave with different backgrounds than those from Manila. *Transregionalism* is a more empirically valid concept for understanding human mobility and does not undercut the importance of stateside entry regulations.

To capture the ways of life in regions and local spaces as well as in whole societies, Hoerder introduced the concept of *"transcultural."* Transcultural approaches to migration between societies, regardless of their territorial extent, connect multiple spaces in which people live and interrelate and which transcend political ("national cultural") boundaries. Transcultural societal studies integrate the traditional discourse-based humanities, the data-based social sciences, the habitus-centered behavioural approaches, the normative disciplines of law, ethics and religion, the life sciences, and the environmental sciences, as well as other fields, into a transdisciplinary whole. Such holistic approaches are required to deal with migrants' whole lives. Transculturalism denotes the competence to live in two or more differing cultures and, in the process, to create a transcultural space which permits moves and linkages back to the evolving space of origin, entry into the evolving space of destination, connections to other spaces, *and* the everyday praxes of *métissage*, fusion, negotiation, conflict, and resistance. Strategic transcultural competence involves capabilities to plan and act life-projects in multiple contexts and to choose. In the process of transculturation, individuals and societies change themselves by integrating diverse lifeways into a new dynamic everyday culture. Subsequent interactions will again change this new – and transitory – culture.[68]

Bibliography

No comprehensive historiographic assessments of the field or generally accepted summaries of theoretical approaches to migrations across the globe have been published.

Lucassen, Jan, and Leo Lucassen, eds, *Migration, Migration History, History: Old Paradigms and New Perspectives* (Bern, 1997; rev. edn, 2007) and Dirk Hoerder, Jan Lucassen, and Leo Lucassen, "Terminologies and Concepts of Migration Research: An Introduction," in Klaus J. Bade, Pieter C. Emmer, Leo Lucassen, and Jochen Oltmer, eds, *Migration – Integration – Minorities since the Seventeenth Century: A European Encyclopaedia* (forthcoming: Cambridge, 2009), provide a summary of approaches to European migrations, theoretical more than historiographical.

"Forum on New Directions in American Immigration and Ethnic History," *Journal of American Ethnic History* 25.4 (2006), 68–167, deals with both historiography and new perspectives as regards the United States. More sociologically oriented is the detailed *Handbook of International Migration: The American Experience*, ed. Charles Hirschman, Philip Kasinitz, and Josh DeWind (New York, 1999). Caroline B. Brettell and James F. Hollifield, eds, *Migration Theory: Talking Across Disciplines* (London, 1999).

Berry, J. W., and J. A. Laponce, eds, *Ethnicity and Culture in Canada: The Research Landscape* (Toronto, 1994), deals extensively with both historiography and new perspectives as regards Canada. Wsevolod W. Isajiw's *Understanding Diversity: Ethnicity and Race in the Canadian Context* (Toronto, 1999) focuses on Canada but is helpful for many societies.

Massey, Douglas S., et al., "Theories of International Migration: Review and Appraisal," *Population and Development Review* 19 (1993), 431–66, and "International Migration Theory: The North American Case," ibid., 20 (1994), 699–752; Dirk Hoerder, "Changing Paradigms in Migration History: From 'To America' to Worldwide Systems," *Canadian Review of American Studies* 24.2

(1994), 105–26, reflect the state of the field in the early 1990s from a Western perspective.

Aspects of theorizing region outside the Western World appear in Ronald Skeldon, *Population Mobility in Developing Countries: A Reinterpretation* (New York, 1990), 27–46, which provides a summary of theoretical approaches, and Mike Parnwell, *Population Movements and the Third World* (London, 1993).

Other attempts at systematizing migrations include James T. Fawcett and Fred Arnold, "Explaining Diversity: Asian and Pacific Immigration Systems," in Fawcett and Benjamin V. Cariño, eds, *Pacific Bridges: The New Immigration from Asia and the Pacific Islands* (Staten Island, NY, 1987), 453–73; A. L. Mabogunje, "Systems Approach to a Theory of Rural–Urban Migration," *Geographical Analysis* 2.1 (1970), 1–18; J. J. Mangolam and H. K. Schwarzweller, "General Theory in the Study of Migration: Current Needs and Difficulties," *International Migration Review* 3 (1968), 3–18.

4
A Systems Approach to Migrant Trajectories

To understand the complexity of agency in local and societal frames and of migrants' trajectories between societies, historians have developed a "systems approach" as a comprehensive theoretical-methodological frame, incorporating the causational and incidental factors and outcomes as well as multiple rationalities.[1] The term should not be confounded with the term "migration systems," introduced by Jan Lucassen to distinguish empirically verifiable patterns of large-scale movement over extended periods of time from minor ones. Lucassen focused on the transregional, Netherlands-centered eighteenth- and nineteenth-century North Sea system; Leslie Page Moch expanded usage to earlier West European migrations, and it has been applied globally since.[2]

A systems approach connects migration decisions and patterns (1) in the society of departure in local, regional, statewide, and global frames, via (2) the actual move across distance, given an era's means of transportation and communication, to (3) the society or societies of destination, again in micro-, meso-, and macro-regional perspectives, and (4) linkages between the communities in which migrants spent or spend part of their lives. A systems approach, applying the interdisciplinarity of transcultural societal studies (chapter 3.8), permits comprehensive analyses of the structures, institutions, and discursive frames of the societies of origin and of arrival, in particular local or regional variants

– including industrialization, urbanization, social stratification, gender roles and family economies, demographic characteristics, political situation and developments, educational
institutions, religious or other belief systems, ethnocultural
composition, and traditions of short- and long-distance
migrations. Interdisciplinary and transcultural approaches
emphasize lived culture and indicate how the interrelated
economic, social, political, and technological forces converge
into a cultural habitus (Bourdieu), a whole way of life
(Raymond Williams), and stimulate migration across space.[3]

 The systems approach analyzes the impact of out-
migration on families and societies of departure and of in-
migration on communities and receiving societies. What was
the impact of the forced departure of millions of enslaved
Africans, or of hundreds of thousands of women from Philippine society today, on each and every family involved (micro-
history), on the region of departure (meso-level), and on
whole societies and macro-regions? What did out-migration
mean for agricultural villages and whole countrysides,
whether in Europe in the late nineteenth century or China in
the late twentieth century? Could plantation societies have
developed without forced, imported workers or core industrialization in Europe and the US without the proletarianizing
migrants from Europe's rural peripheries? How did the
migrating men and women negotiate the cultural change and
necessary adjustment? How would families in the highly
developed World of the present take care of children and the
elderly without migrant women from Bangladesh or Mexico?
Societies and economies have been and are linked globally
through families spread across several countries. The decisions of millions of men and women to migrate changes
communities and societies of origin as much as those in which
they decide to establish a transitory or permanent home.

The systems approach, based on migrant agency within
structural constraints, needs to be modified for involuntary
migrants such as forced, indentured, or enslaved workers, as
well as for refugees. These are deprived of agency at the time
of departure. Their post-migration survival and insertion,
however, depends on choices, if under severely constraining
conditions. Slave acculturation resulted in African-origin cultures in the Americas and elsewhere. Refugees need to insert

themselves into labour markets, whether they be Vietnamese in Hong Kong or German Jews in 1930s Turkey. Forced labourers in camps in Nazi Germany, Stalinist Russia, or South Africa first had to struggle for pure survival and then, once liberated, to rebuild lives.

Migration has often been dealt with as a move between two societies, and we will discuss it as such to facilitate understanding of the factors involved. However, moves may involve stopovers or may lead on from a first destination to other societies or, after time, back to the society of origin. Each subsequent move involves new processes of adjustment, and a return demands reinsertion into a community that has evolved and changed during the migrant's absence.

4.1 Structures and Agency: Contextualizing Migration Decisions

When people begin to consider whether to migrate or not, they have completed the formative socialization period of their lives, intra-family childhood and societal-educational adolescence. They have become part of communities of kin, region, and state. In this process, which is specific by status or class and by gender, and in some societies by race, the young learn and internalize the practices and values of their elders and of the society as a whole. It is also specific to region: people speak with particular accents, eat particular foods, and act in particular landscapes. Such space is invested with meaning according to class and gender as well as ethno-culture and race. Working- and middle-class people live in different quarters; peasant families and large landowners appropriate space differently; women face restrictions on mobility different from men. In hierarchized multiracial societies, children may be imbued with racist frames of mind or be told from infancy on that they are inferior. For each group, the geographic landscape becomes a specific "socio-scape," open or delimited, within which decisions are made to stay or to depart.

The processual structures in which socialization and decision-making occur involve, most intensively, the micro-level of family and community. Since cultural practices and economic opportunities vary by region, this meso-level also impacts on migrant decisions. On the macro-level of statewide institutions, migrants need to take into account limitations on exit, procedures for arranging the trip, and entry regulations at the destination. Nineteenth-century Tamil migrants to plantations in Ceylon (now Sri Lanka) departed from regions in southern British India with their specific cultural-economic characteristics. English migrants from London are different from people hailing from Bristol; individuals from rural Sussex from those of industrialized Lancashire. Twentieth-century Congolese migrants, like many others, differ by ethnoculture and urban or rural origin. Only in the societies of arrival, where their new neighbours are unable to distinguish such cultural differentiation, are migrants labelled as generic English Americans or Indian Tamils or other.

Socialization provides people with their human capital, i.e. their individual capabilities, and the gendered and status-specific social environment provides them with social capital, i.e. connections to others and to societal resources. The combination of human and social capital permits each and every individual to fashion a scape (Appadurai), a person- and group-specific social landscape for him- or herself. Young people construct scapes distinct from those of adults; women's scapes are different from those of men; non-moving producers view and live markets differently than mobile traders.

The micro-environment of potential migrants, i.e. the (extended or truncated) family and neighbourhood networks, is embedded in worldviews and information linkages. As regards interpretations of the world, some religions taught people to be content with their station and wait to be rewarded in another world. Adherents of such faiths have to secularize their aspirations and hopes in order to increase options, either by struggling to improve the society of their birth or to improve their individual lives by migration to another society and community-formation there. To make such choices, people need information: the micro-scapes of their actual lives are connected to distant micro-scapes where kin and friends have gone: information usually comes from trusted earlier migrants. Emigrant guides, agencies' advertising, or government recruitment were often viewed sceptically, since potential migrants could not establish their trustworthiness but surmised specific interests of the authors. For example, women working in urban middle-class households, whether regional migrants in nineteenth-century Berlin or Somali women in twenty-first-century Rome, establish such information linkages and networks. They provide potential migrants with mental maps and permit assessment of options available.

While a frequently used cliché has them depart to the "unlimited opportunities" of a nineteenth-century America or a twentieth-century industrialized Singapore or Canada, migrants carefully evaluate information and compare options, since their limited means do not permit experimentation. Problems occur when societal-mental frames of reference cannot decode the news arriving from other cultures and economies. In the late nineteenth century, the news that in America trains travelled over the roofs of houses – like birds – seemed to indicate unlimited technological possibilities, though it merely described elevated trains in New York or Chicago. Similarly, in the late twentieth century, radio and television images of "the wealthy West," of urban South Asia in Bollywood, or of towering skyscrapers in Shanghai, reflect middle- or upper-class standards of living unobtainable by migrants with but few skills and resources. The glossy images show neither labour market statistics nor discrimination. Influenced by both the information and the images of better life-course options, potential migrants throughout the ages have considered it unfair to families, children, and themselves not to strive to improve their condition.

Migration research explores selectivity: How, from a pool of potential migrants, do the particular individuals and families who actually leave select themselves or become selected? Societal structures, individual human capital, family economies, and social capital set parameters. Structural factors include inheritance and dowry-giving or bride-price patterns, as well as patterns of gifting at birth or burial and, for young men, impending military service. Such age-related factors are more closely related to departure decisions than general insufficiency of jobs or land, of options, and of income security. In families, sibling sequence and culturally mandated roles, e.g. responsibility for the care of aging parents, are further factors. In tradition-ruled societies, norm-breaking and problematic personal relationships – courtship not approved by parents, unsuccessful love affairs, child-birth out of wedlock, or offences against laws – increase the propensity of individuals to leave.[4] The inclination to depart increases when a death, usually of a parent, or the remarriage of a widowed parent imposes a restructuring of emotional relationships. Gender impacts: the death of a mother or the arrival of a stepmother influences departure more than death or departure of a father. Young people, who account for the majority of migrants, experience multiple changes which exert a cumulative influence on the decision to leave home: passage from youth to adulthood; capability to support oneself and to found a family; impending rupture because of military or domestic service elsewhere.

In regions with few options, out-migration was or is a customary or even a compulsory way of life; the mental topography accepts migration as "normal." In societies of the present, in which lives have become more individualized and family context less important, the individual aspects of decision-making increase but remain connected to social networks and information flows.

4.2 The Society of Departure

If people act in their own perceived best interest, they do so within conditions not of their own making but set by historical development and actual power structures. Agency is reduced for forced migrants to a struggle for survival, and for refugees to a reordering of their disrupted lives. Among voluntary migrants, in addition to intergenerational issues, gender roles, family economies, and community belongings discussed in chapter 4.1, society-wide frames of action include industrialized and urban labour markets, demography and stratification, and authoritarian or participatory political systems, as well as schooling opportunities and normative systems. A society's ethnocultural composition and hierarchies as well as traditions of short- and long-distance migrations also impact on propensity to migrate.

The systems approach places societies in the global hierarchization of domination, development, and dependency. People depart from societies whose economy does not provide sufficient options to earn a living or whose rigid stratification prevents them from exploring the reach of their human capital. Repressive regimes and past-oriented socio-political structures, targeting a religious practice or ethnic culture as well as a specific gender or generation, induce departures. Job-generating investments often advantage the state's dominant ethnocultural and ethno-religious group or groups. Women may decide to leave because societies of destination impose fewer restraints on them; if unmarried, they may be pushed out because they are considered a non-productive burden on society, as in late nineteenth-century Great Britain or in parts of China.

During the so-called demographic transition, when population growth and economic growth do not match, families and young people leave in large numbers. Infant survival rates and life expectation of adults increase, but birth rates per couple do not yet decline and labour markets do not yet expand. An increasing percentage of young people find no opportunity to earn their living. This transition occurred in Europe in the later nineteenth century and is occurring in many Arab, African, and Asian societies in the present. People correct such demographic–economic imbalances by migrating from spaces with a surplus of livelihood-seeking men and women to those with a demand for additional workers. Such migration, a "mobility transition," involves an interregional or global process of balancing supply with demand, options with resources.[5] Patterns of migration are, usually, interregional and intra-state rural–urban before they become international. Once a society's expanding labour market provides sufficient options for wage work, departure rates decline.

Stratification and rigid class structures that prevent upward mobility encourage departures – or militancy: struggles for improving the society of one's birth and out-migration reflect different strategies. Some men and women join reform movements, such as labour unions or political parties, to improve in a collective manner unsatisfactory conditions at home. Others individually seek to enhance their personal or family condition by moving to better options and more flexibly structured societies. Such structures, quantifiable in research, are assessed by migrants in their feedback to friends and kin: hard work and achievements count, job applicants do not have to cringe or pay bribes, domestics are treated well, employers rectify grievances. Expectations were not always fulfilled. East European immigrant workers in the late nineteenth-century United States were as dissatisfied with their treatment as West African migrants in France or peasant newcomers in China's cities are in the present.

Long-term traditions of mobility facilitate departures, since potential migrants may rely on information and, often, on guides. People travelling from Hong Kong to San Francisco or Vancouver, from Bremen to New York or Galveston, or from the Philippines to the Persian Gulf follow clearly demarcated routes, whether the markers are printed or oral. The self-reinforcing attractiveness of migration systems emerged from the information generated and easily accessible. Distances to be traversed, cultural affinities, possibilities (and the cost) of regular return, and congruence of skills and job openings inform migration decisions rather than imagined wealth.

While societal arrangements and processes always impacted on migration, the roles of states changed dramatically from the control of emigration to the control of immigration. Emigration regulations or prohibitions were the practice in many dynastic states to the mid-nineteenth century, longer in China and Japan (and in communist societies before 1989). State-side departure regulations attempt to keep stationary the internal labour reservoir and wage levels and are concerned with tax revenues, with military service in the case of men, and with the threat of independent decision-making in the case of women. Potential migrants had to apply for permission to leave. Gender-specific rules framed the mobility of women more than that of men. In the present, some states regulate women's out-migration to domestic and caregiving work in an attempt to harness their wage remittances to fiscal policies.

In the nineteenth century and before, colonizer states imposed mobility on colonized societies to acquire labourers as commodities. Emigration control "at home" might thus be paralleled by enforced out-migration in the colonies. In the Atlantic World, states took charge of the options available to young people by nationalizing educational systems. If, for nationalist reasons, these systematically disadvantage people of particular dialects or "minority" cultures, the propensity to migrate increases.

Since the late nineteenth century, immigration controls replaced emigration controls first in the Atlantic World. The "invention of the passport" (Torpey) changed a travel document into an instrument of national identification and allegiances. Instead of being a permit to pass a port of entry, it became an instrument to exclude those of other cultures or colours of skin.[6] It took decades until such controls could be fully enforced. Asian migrants were excluded from North America in the 1880s; for Europeans regulations were tightened, but near-exclusion came only in the 1920s. Patrols along the US–Mexican border, initiated in the mid-1920s, were to prevent a "browning" of the US population. In Europe, passport laws were operationalized faster. As a side-effect, in the 1930s they made flight from fascist states difficult, as entry was denied to refugees without papers. Rigorous immigration control laws and visa procedures reached new heights in the second half of the twentieth century. Many of these measures were directed against the people living in the independent states that had once been colonized by Britain, France, Portugal, or the United States – and who were of skin colour other than white.

The colonial and, from the mid-nineteenth century, imperial outreach furthered state-supported investments abroad as well as military conquest of agricultural lands, industrial centers, or regions providing raw materials. Such power-mediated opportunities, whether in mining, oil extraction, or other sectors, stimulated migration of the respective state's nationals to the occupied territories. British capital exports globally, Japanese railroad building in Manchuria, US investment in the Caribbean, and French control of West Africa induced outbound migration of "nationals" and mobilized "locals" to labour for the investor-colonizers. The resulting core–periphery hierarchy and the differential standards of living have the unintended consequences of inducing men and women from dependent economies to migrate to the core.

States and societies with high rates of out-migration change in consequence. In the phase of the demographic and mobility transition, emigration might decrease pressure on labour markets and permit wages to rise and standards of living to improve. Societies might become more stable. Policy-makers and administrators, however, often feared loss of tax revenues, army recruits, and women able to bear children for the state. The social cost of emigration, on the other hand, was not discussed at the time. Families and societies "invest" in raising and educating children, who do not yet contribute to family income or tax revenues. On reaching taxpaying age, this new generation "repays" intra-family and intra-societal investment in an intergenerational transfer of the cost of caring for "dependents," i.e. the young and the old. This "compact between generations" remains unfulfilled if people withdraw by emigration from the obligation to support the elderly – their parents – and the next generation. Working-age migrants take their accumulated individual and social capital with them. The state of their birth cannot recover social costs, while the state of destination benefits from their taxes and productivity and gets trained and educated men and women "for free." This impact has been called "development aid" by poorer societies for those that are more developed.

Some states attempt to rid themselves of people considered "undesirable," whether political or religious dissidents, "the poor," underemployed proletarians, or people considered deficient for other reasons. Examples are many: the deportation of dissidents and criminals from Russia to Siberia and of paupers and criminals from Western Europe to America and Australia; Great Britain's program of shipping off unmarried women and orphaned children; deportations by the US of alleged socialists and revolutionaries during the "Red Scare" (or "white fear") around 1920, and by China of dissidents in the present. States and economic elites may also force people to depart because of institutionalized capital–labour relations that do not provide acceptable working and wage conditions. Around 2000, for example, Mexico's inequality ratio (the ratio of income of the top 10 percent of the population to the bottom 10 percent) stood at 32.6, as compared to 16.6 in the US and 8.5 in Canada.

Similarly, before the 1880s, the inequality rate in Europe was far higher than in the US. In such cases, people leave for the less hierarchical society.

It has been argued that states lose their most active or most dynamic population through out-migration. Such a statement, difficult to prove, is based on the assumption that only dynamic and highly qualified men and women are capable of navigating the process of change between societies. However, along established migration routes people travel easily and develop a migration habitus. States with living conditions unacceptable to many often face high departure rates of the professionally trained and of men and women considered less dynamic; the dictatorial regimes in Latin America or in Africa in the 1980s may serve as examples.

To summarize, societies of departure are undergoing uneven internal development. Resulting out-migration changes them by depriving them of part of the human capital – if often an unusable capital given the stage of development. Out-migration may reduce the need to create jobs or to reform constraining structures. Migrants send back money and thus contribute both to their family's budget and to the state's foreign currency reserves. Large sections of some sending states' budgets, from those of nineteenth-century Italy to the late twentieth-century Philippines, have depended and depend on migrant women's and men's remittances. While some economists and politicians have extolled investment opportunities provided by such transfers, the recipient families often need these funds to prevent consumption patterns from sliding below subsistence level. In slightly better circumstances, they use the money to improve consumption and status. Still, unless durable consumer goods need to be imported, such transfers improve a state's balance of payments. Migrants may also transfer ideas, through communication or following return in person, and the resulting innovation may improve a stagnant economy. But elites benefiting from the old state of affairs often oppose the infusion of new ideas and practices or prevent them altogether. Since the age of fascism, whole modern states have been refugee-generating apparatuses. Political elites lose the trust of large segments of the society, as in El Salvador or in Pinochet's Chile. Economically weak but resource-rich states such as the

Congo may become the prey of global investors and thereby lose sustainable social and ecological structures. In such worst-case scenarios, emigration becomes a survival strategy. Voluntary migration, in contrast, often is a strategy better to invest human and social capital into life-course projects. States and societies need to provide institutional-cultural environments that permit sustainable lives.[7]

4.3   Voyages: Extended, Compressed, Delayed

In the past, migrants' mental-geographical maps structured distances and places by days travelled on foot, by cart, by railroad, or by ship. In the present, the cost of air travel and the number of time zones traversed are important. Departure involves a mental weaning from the community of origin, a separation from kin and friends. By this time, the myths and information about the destination have been formed into a set of personal hopes and expectations. The actual inter-regional or intersocietal move involves obstacles and inducements.

Obstacles include the cost of the voyage, which needs to be related to the days, months, or years of work it takes to save this amount. Voyaging also means that, during this, formerly extended, period, no income may be earned. Emigration regulations may pose barriers and immigration restrictions almost insurmountable ones. Racial bars erected in the Anglo-American and European societies against men and women from Asia and other "people of colour" in the later nineteenth century made entry difficult. Racist exclusion lasted to the 1960s in North America – longer in Europe – and still characterizes Japan's immigration rules. Nineteenth-century contract labourers sometimes encountered dishonest recruiting agents, and from the late twentieth century both migrants without entry permits and women face traffickers.

Among inducements are prepaid tickets sent by earlier migrants or, in the case of the indentured migrants from Asia, contractually guaranteed return fares. They also include accurate information on the trip and the availability of income-generating positions after arrival. Finally, prior migration experience helps navigate the routes and means of transportation: 12 percent of all Europeans arriving in the US from 1899 to 1910 had been there before (in other words, every eighth traveller could act as guide for others).

Travel arrangements are made on the basis of information sent by prior migrants and with the help of guides from the community. Pioneer migrants had to rely on sailors or long-distance merchants or, from the 1830s on, on railway personnel. For centuries, "travel agencies" arranged package tours. Medieval pilgrims destined for Jerusalem would make their way to Venice and book a passage across the Mediterranean. Arranged pilgrimages were as common in other faiths; the Muslim *hajj* is the best example. Such extended voyaging involves transformations, de- and resocializations as regards identities, self-definition, and community integration.[8] During the extended transoceanic voyages in the period of sail – in the early fifteenth-century Asian seas and the Indian Ocean as much as in the mid-nineteenth-century transpacific and transatlantic travel – migrants had to adjust to shipboard food and to mass quarters. On board, anxieties about destinations and hopes or life-projects could be shared, discussed, amended, and expanded or reduced. Young migrants formed communities of ship "brothers" and "sisters."

Travel accelerated with the introduction of railroads in the 1830s and sea-going steamships in the 1870s. From the mid-nineteenth century, migrants across Europe contracted with the local representative of a reliable agency connected to the distant shipping and railroad companies. Contract labourers in India or China would approach a recruiting office that would also take charge of the trip. Change of trains and embarkation was done under supervision of the agencies' personnel – the voyage was as organized as modern group tourism. Voyaging became even more time-compressed with air travel from the mid-1950s on. To take one example, domestics migrating in the 1970s from Guyana to Canada had only their keen observation to navigate airport procedures alien to them and had to insert themselves into Toronto life a few hours later.

Some migrants move stepwise, first as far as their limited funds take them – for example to a job-providing city, ideally the one with the port or airport of future departure. For some, the need to earn money for the next leg of the trip is an unwelcome delay, for others a welcome stopover for a first adjustment. Travel experiences and emotional coping vary individually. To gauge demands placed on migrants we need to be aware that many nineteenth-century migrants had never seen a train or a ship before they stepped aboard – just as many twentieth-century migrants had never been on a plane or Vietnamese refugee "boat people" and West and North African trans-Mediterranean boat-transported labour migrants neither had seafaring experience nor knew how to swim. At all times, the voyage itself meant a speeding-up of lives which might stop short, unintentionally, at a border fence and slow to weeks or months of waiting. Accounts reflect both easygoing confidence and bewilderment.

Since the later twentieth century, states' territorial borders have changed meaning and place. International borders are encumbrances experienced in airport basements somewhere within a county or outside its borders in visa-granting or -refusing consulates. Powerful states impose control at perimeters distant from their borders, at extra-territorial US immigration checkpoints in Hong Kong or Toronto airports, for example. Powerful states externalize borders: the EU demands control of northbound West African migrants at Algeria's southern border, the US of Latin American migrants at Mexico's southern border. Such control systems interrupt customary local transborder migrations and, from such disrupted economies, further (often non-white) migrants have to depart for the exclusion-practicing states of the First, often implicitly white, World.

International borders or, in some societies – present-day China, for example – rules for admission to a city are important only for those who lack entry permits or whose status is within the assumed meaning of those entry rules but does not conform to them to the letter, and thus may result in lengthy detention and interrogation. Since the late nineteenth-century imposition of immigration controls, admission procedures have been fraught with fears of rejection. In the view of migrants, even the US rules, liberal for migrants from Asia to the early 1880s and for those from Europe to 1917, were difficult to negotiate because of frequent administrative changes, lack of precise information, and sometimes abusive treatment. While before 1914 the US restrictions excluded less than 5 percent of those intending to enter from Europe, they did tear apart families if some members were admitted and others were sent back. They impacted on larger numbers in disconcerting and gendered ways, as when women travelling alone were suspected of being prostitutes or when men, who had pre-arranged workplaces to be able to support themselves, would be rejected as contract labourers.

In the late twentieth century, entry rules in most states, even those admitting immigrants, became highly restrictive. People without the means to support themselves, traumatized refugees, those with emotional scars from political persecution, face rejection. Rejection began in the 1930s when the refugee-generating fascist states were surrounded by refugee-refusing democracies. During the Cold War, the West welcomed refugees from communist countries but refused admission to those from right-wing dictatorships or from Third World countries. Since then, a system of "global apartheid" closes entry-gates for vast numbers of refugees, whether from Vietnam, from Chile, or from African countries. Their involuntary voyages are delayed. They are stacked away in camps that "house" or "warehouse" tens of thousands. For people voyaging with the problems of their past and without means, borders remain closed.

To ever larger numbers, undocumented entry provides a last hope. However, the crossing of the seas – from post-1975 Vietnam, from Haiti in the 1980s, or from North or West Africa in the present – is often deadly. Those who survive but are apprehended face forced return, *"refoulement,"* to the society of origin. Still, millions have entered countries of the northern hemisphere without the required travel documents and either are forced to live clandestine lives as *sans-papiers*, or "undocumented," or are criminalized as "illegals," as in 1990s US discourse. They are people without papers but with aspirations and, usually, a will to work hard, living "at the border called hope."[9]

It is worth recalling that the hopeful and strategizing colonizers from Europe and America in the previous centuries also came without valid papers of the society they intended to enter and to annex, exploit, or take over: what if the

"Pilgrims" at Plymouth Rock or the British opium importers in Hong Kong had needed entry permits from the native Massachusetts chieftains or from Guangdong administrators?

4.4   The Receiving Society: Economic Insertion, Acculturation, Politics, and New Belongings

As regards receiving societies, the systems approach replaces older "ethnic group" narratives by analyses of migrant agency in complex structures and processes.[10] In the decades around 1900, nationalist politicians and scholars assumed that newcomers could be reprogrammed under "Americanization," "Germanization," "Sinicization," or similar projects and programs. Such ideological positions have been questioned since the 1930s transculturation theories (chapter 3.3). The debilitating flaw of assimilation approaches is the assumption of a single and unchanging mainstream or national receiving culture. Though, in the present, some states still mandate a "become like us" course, we need to remember that data on population composition in the 1990s indicated that in only one-fifth of the world's states did the largest ethnic group – the so-called nation – account for more than 90 percent of the population. In almost one-third, the hegemonic group accounted for less than three-quarters of the population. Receiving societies provide no single model of acculturation; migrants have to make choices reflecting societally accepted gender positioning, social status, regional specifics, and legal frames.

"Race" complicates acculturation trajectories, since people of colours other than white have generally not been accepted as equal in the white North Atlantic societies; nor are Koreans treated as equal in Japan or people of darker phenotypes in India. The allegedly all-pervasive beauty of "white" may appear as mere pigment-deprived paleness, as in "paleface." All such phenotypical characterizations have been constructed over time in particular contexts and from particular interests. In "white" societies, structural and attitudinal discrimination have forced other-than-white migrants into distinct und unequal positions. While Canada and the US abolished race-based immigrant admission criteria in the 1960s, the long history of racism in the US still constrains options of African Americans and of newcomers from African backgrounds. In European countries, the arrival of people from the former colonies and the southern hemisphere as a whole has resulted in new racisms (see chapter 5.1 below).

People, regardless of colour, gender, or class, arrive fully socialized. They are called the migrant or first generation.[11] Their children, the second generation, have been called "ethnics" or of "ethnocultural" or "migrant" background. When whole families leave, as in the refugee movement from Iran for example, partly socialized adolescent children continue their education in the receiving society. This special group has been called a "1.5 generation." The grandchildren of migrants are counted as third generation. Most research shows acculturation processes to extend over three generations. Some studies indicate that educated, cosmopolitan middle-class or internationalist-minded working-class migrants acculturate in a shorter time. In contrast, groups that are racialized or otherwise marginalized may be prevented from becoming part of the mainstream for many generations or even centuries – Koreans in Japan, Turks in Germany, African-Americans in the US are examples. While majority opinion often ascribes social marginality to individual migrants' inability or inferiority, comparative research on migrants from the same origin, for example Turks in Germany, Great Britain, and the US, indicates the decisive role of the insertion regime. Structural openness or closedness determines options for participating far more than ethnocultural "traits" or preferences.

Migrants usually do not consciously move into a state, nation, or political system but rather to perceived opportunities according to their cultural, especially linguistic, affinities. Entrepreneurial and investor migrants excepted, most arrive with very limited resources and economic insertion is their first and foremost goal. Ideally, they may select a labour market segment suitable to their skills, i.e. their human capital; more often they have to enter segments with a high availability of jobs and low demand by resident workers ("nationals") because of poor wages and working conditions.

Once they secure their basic daily sustenance and necessities, they begin to deal with local and regional social life in a second stage. Most turn to politics and show an interest in statewide institutions in a last, third, stage.

"Acculturation" is a double process: a stepwise approach by the migrant to the new society or specific segments of it while retaining some elements of the culture of socialization, modifying others, and discarding yet others; and an often reluctant or belated adaptation of the receiving society to the newcomers. "Insertion" refers to migrants' functioning in an economic (or other) niche from which they may explore further aspects of the new environment. "Accommodation" and "adjustment" refer to a negotiated change of some cultural practices to expand contacts with the receiving society while retaining other practices. The concept of "acculturation," best suited to understand migrant experiences, involves a continuous negotiating between views and practices acquired during the socialization in the culture of origin and the exigencies of the receiving community in specific segments such as workplace, schools, or neighbourhood. To discuss acculturation processes in terms of segments helps to isolate those in which participation is achieved easily from those in which conflict, problems, or exclusion occurs. Unsatisfactory integration demands analyses of problem-producing structures and attitudes. Unexpectedly low achievement and skill attainment levels of children of some migrant groups in specific societies since the 1980s need to be analyzed in terms of access to schooling, and their low labour market performance may result from deindustrialization in which whole labour market segments, suited to their qualifications, vanish.

The economic sphere, in which migrants need to operate from arrival, is characterized by segmented, stratified, and segregated labour markets (see chapter 3.6). For business and investor migrants, insertion involves a search for a sector in which their capabilities and capital may best be utilized. For migrants into domestic labour and, far more so, caregiving tasks, fast familiarization with the intimate sphere of family life as well as language competency is required. In contrast to US-style rags-to-riches myths, "success" means an income, gained usually by hard work, that permits individuals to sustain themselves or contribute to the family economy. It refers to a modest life according to individuals' preferences, given their means.

In the economic sphere, the interests of the receiving society and the newcomers meet: the former wants men and women who function in sectors with a shortage of labour supply, the latter want to earn a living. This conjuncture of interests causes states to open entry-gates otherwise closed and migrants to fulfil some of their goals, if not under conditions of their own choosing. If easily segregable groups are admitted, such regulation of entry may permit employers to exploit newcomers in racialized and segregated settings.

Migrants explore the new social environment first in the neighbourhood – usually a low-rent area of a city or a suburb with people of many cultural backgrounds or an ethnic enclave. Over time, they extend their reach to the larger city and region and, perhaps, to society-wide institutions and practices. Migrants generally do not target one city from a wide rage of cities as their destination but rather particular neighbourhoods and locations where acquaintances and kin settled earlier, provide an anchor point, and translate between old and new cultural ways. Sequential migration often brings in kin and friends with earning capacities first in order to strengthen the economic basis. In the selection of who moves, affectionate ties have to rank lower, since limited social capital and lack of savings make support for small children or elderly parents impossible. Patterns of sequential migration are gendered. Men establish predominantly male migration chains; women tend to send for sisters and female friends. Migration truncates families often for long periods of time – transnational family relationships emerge (see chapter 5.3 below).

In both the economic and the social sphere, migrants frequently experience discrimination. While race and culture are major factors, migrants often appear as generally uncouth or dumb to resident nationals because they express emotions and interests in their own spoken and body language and with other registers: thus they seem incapable of communicating like "everybody" else. Bilingualism on both sides could defuse such conflict-prone non-understanding. Knowledge of the receiving society's language is a distinct advantage – thus the migrations from regions once colonized by the French,

Dutch, or English states to the societies of former imperial domination. Employers' personnel managers with more than one language may facilitate migrant hiring in the interest both of their firm and of the newly arrived job applicants.

Migrants may improve their bargaining power by increasing their numbers and developing quantitative clout and by organizing. Thus insertion and acculturation processes depend to some degree on group size and length of stay in the new society. Organization involves mutual aid in the migration context, linkages to the community of origin, and support for adaptation of cultural practices. Labour unions in some receiving societies recruit migrants; in others they exclude them as (racially) inferior or unlettered. Immigrant communities and the receiving society interact in the workplace and in educational and other institutions. Over time – measured in years or generations – such interactions become increasingly dense, the actors progressively responsive or acculturated to each other.

Development and intensity of interaction depend both on the participatory options a receiving society offers and on the willingness of migrants to avail themselves of such options or to struggle to expand them. In an intergenerational perspective, educational institutions are of particular importance. Are schools as institutions accessible to migrant children? Is the content of particular lessons meaningful to and useful for them? Do immigrant parents want education for their children – a cost factor in family budgets – or do they want the children to work and contribute to family income? This intergenerational aspect of acculturation is shaped by family strategies and the receiving society's educational institutions and participatory policies, if any. In scholarship, traditional emphasis on immigrant adults is being supplemented by research on youth in transcultural and multicultural settings.[12]

The more active creation of and participation by women in networks may involve both a larger loss of connectivity upon departure and a particularly important role in community formation and contact with neighbours after arrival. In numerous migrant-attracting societies women encounter fewer gender-specific role constraints, and thus their propensity for return migration is lower than that of men. Their increased educational options and labour force participation provide receiving societies with a comparative advantage, as regards the rate of gainfully employed to dependent segments of the population, over societies which place restrictions on education and waged work of women (see chapter 5.2).

In the migrants' own comparative analysis of their two (or more) societies – as revealed in interviews, letters, and other life-writings – the selected receiving society provides increased options and, often, is characterized by less rigid stratification. In some societies, however, migrants – similar to resident "minorities" – are slotted into a permanent underclass position from which they cannot escape. Scholars have called this intersection of class and ethnoculture an eth-class regime.

The assumption that migrants achieve a higher standard of living in developing societies, such as the US in the past or South Korea in the present, demands careful analysis. It is premised on higher wage levels but usually does not factor in migrant segregation into low-paying labour market segments or higher costs of living (see chapter 3.2 above). Complex research needs to include both economic and social institutions, comparing, in addition to wages and cost of living, social services and recreational opportunities. Late nineteenth-century British emigrants left economies with low wages but acceptable social services for higher wages in the US but deprivation of social services. Rural migrants, moving from a tiny but sanitary village accommodation to Manchuria, Argentina, or the North American plains often ended up in shacks or dugouts. For many, migration involved a downward slide and an improved standard of living only after years of hard work or in the second generation. Urban migrants moving from tenements in a European, Asian, or African city to cheap quarters in Nairobi, New York, Paris, Moscow, or Shanghai often merely exchange one underserviced and run-down neighbourhood for another. Life in a *favela* in Rio de Janeiro or a *gececondu* in Istanbul is intended as a step to expected increased options but involves an actual decrease in the standard of living. Lasting downswings in global economic cycles may extend such downward mobility for decades.

As regards the third sphere of acculturation, involvement in statewide politics, self-organization in immigrant neighbourhoods provides a first level of participation. From activity in the immediate neighbourhood, participation may extend to an urban or rural district, and finally expand to include the countrywide level. Open institutional regimes encourage migrant inclusion and participation; closed ones may result in ghettoization, alienation, and conflict. Structures that cause migrants' life-courses and plans to deviate may generate behaviour viewed as "deviant" by the very society that sends newcomers into such trajectories. Access to political decision-making, i.e. participatory involvement, research shows, is far more effective for migrant integration and feelings of belonging than a host society's distant "respect" for or mere "tolerance" of cultural difference. Interactive participation demands that residents understand migrants' interests and lifeways and that migrants come to terms with the receiving society's institutions (see chapter 6.2 and 6.3).

An empirically grounded, US-specific theory of integration was proposed by Milton Gordon in the context of the 1960s discussion of race and racialization. He discussed race and intermarriage, religion, and ethno-national origin, as well as absence of prejudice and discrimination (attitude and behaviour receptional assimilation on the part of the receiving society).[13] Canadian sociologists John Goldlust and Anthony Richmond tested a more differentiated multivariate model of immigrant adaptation. The Norwegian anthropologist Fredrik Barth focused on "ethnic groups" and their assumed culture and demonstrated how, through negotiations along boundaries and institutional interactions, groups constantly shape and reshape their identities and images.[14] The process of entering a society, itself many faceted and evolving, involves (1) the segmented acculturation discussed above; (2) structural acculturation in the triple sense of access, equal participation in decision-making, and adaptability of institutions and (processual) structures; and (3) identificational acculturation in the sense that newcomers consider themselves and are considered part of society. Upon entry the migrants bring their human capital, their social capital, and their savings or investment capital. The last may be transferred most easily. Human capital is transferred as part of the individual but may not be useful in the new social and economic conditions. Social capital, networks, and access to resources are most difficult to transfer – thus sequential migrations between networks assume high importance for acculturation.

Identification implies "embeddedness" in community, social practices, and institutions. The concept of "belonging" is premised on equality, connectivity, and participation and counters political theorizations that accept as given marginalization, racialization, and fragmentation. This concept also views states and societies as constantly adapting and adaptable.[15]

Recognizing the shortcomings of the traditional political theory of territorially limited nation-states and emphasizing a citizenship based on human rights regardless of gender, ethnoculture, race, or class, Tariq Modood and Veit Bader have proposed models of societal organization that would not merely attempt to tie immigrants to existing structures but would connect transnational spaces and the people living in them. On the basis both of recognition of diversity in history and of social and political cohesion based on equality of all members, "democratic institutional pluralism" in a "moderately, rather than a radically, secular state" would permit recognition, integration, and – most importantly – participation of many-cultured transnational migrants, accept their spiritual beliefs, and permit associational life. Traditional postulates of institutions' "difference-blind neutrality . . . [tend] to stabilize existing structural (economic, social, political) and cultural or symbolic *inequalities* between majorities and minorities." Institutional pluralism – ideally as "associative democracy" – is able "to find productive balances between the collective autonomy of minorities and individual autonomy." For individuals, it "develops real exit options (not only exit rights) and is based on overlapping and crosscutting membership in many associations." "Politics of recognition" needs to dissolve "the institutional separation between private faith and public authority" because "a strict public/private distinction may simply act to buttress the privileged position of historically 'integrated' folk cultures at the expense of historically *subordinated* or newly migrated folk." To illustrate this with a case in point: the French state is premised on separation of state and religion. Thus Muslim girls have been forbidden to wear the *hijab* in public schools.

But the state recognizes and enforces Christian holidays. The rhetoric of neutrality veils the privileges of Christian French.[16]

Such theorization based on recognition of the historicity of migration and of state structures, and on cultural interaction and economic frames, involves an interdisciplinary systems approach to complex societies. It replaces narrow political science studies of particularly powerful mainstream groups called "nation" and of the "state" as its central organization. The systems approach to complex and changing polities is not limited to two (or more) societies and the migratory connections between them but incorporates continuing transcultural linkages.

4.5   Global Interdependence and Transcultural Lives

Transnationality or, better, transculturation is part of the experience of each and every society on the globe. Many-cultured societies in which people transcended borders include the Muslim–Jewish–Christian ones on the Iberian peninsula from the tenth to the twelfth century and the Muslim–Hindu ones in South Asia from the tenth century. In the fifteenth-century Indian Ocean World, commercial migrants connected ports and, wherever stopping over, could administer their own quarters. The Ottoman Empire, from the fourteenth to the seventeenth century, with its vast variety of ethno-religiously defined peoples, institutionalized coexistence through supra-cultural governmental institutions and practices. In such societies, communities were bordered, but borders were permeable and connections to communities elsewhere intensive. To capture such transborder connectivity, historians have reduced emphasis on territorial-political rule in order to study the interconnected systems of the Mediterranean World, the World of the Indian Ocean, or traditional diasporas – for example those of the Chinese or the Jews or, more recently, of the Scots, the Italians, the Poles, or the Lebanese. Economic historians have always dealt with, for instance, cotton and cloth or grain production across the globe and have included the producers, whether residing locally, migrating voluntarily, or, as slaves, being forced to migrate.

The nineteenth-century transoceanic migrations in the Atlantic, Indian Ocean, and Asian Seas' Worlds as well as across the Pacific have been recognized as involving long-lasting linkages between people (still) in the societies of departure and those (already) settled in the receiving societies. Transoceanic family and community lives were the rule in the so-called age of nation-states, when 90 percent or more of migrants joined kin and friends who had migrated earlier. Around 1900, tens of millions of letters annually provided information from the US to all of Europe's communities of origin. In the Asian contract labour system and across the Pacific, return and multiple migrations connected communities. Remittances connected families across the oceans, as did the usually overlooked transfer of inheritances from societies of origin to immigrant children; to the early 1870s, more such funds were transferred to the US than remittances sent from there. Migrants requested flower and vegetable seeds from their countries of birth to achieve aesthetic and culinary continuity in their home of choice. Life-writings document such transcultural continuities as well as their waning over time.[17]

Forced migrations either made transcultural connections seemingly impossible or rigorously constrained them. But owners of the enslaved could not deprive their human property of the internalized culture carried to the destinations. Slave and free Africans connected the many societies of the black Atlantic; indentured workers from Indian or Chinese regional societies created ways of life in the world's plantation belt. While written exchanges between the often illiterate forced migrants may have been limited, we need to keep in mind that, in oral cultures, non-written memory is highly developed – but it is not easily traceable for historians.

"Transnational" connections, in the literal meaning, may emerge only once nation-states come into existence. While US proponents of the concept have assumed such connections to be, in fact, only a post-1980s phenomenon, British scholars have preferred the concept of diaspora, with its deep historicity, for the same connections. The research of the last decade and a half indicates that, "Historically, transnational connections, cultures and communities were the 'normal' state of affairs. This ubiquitous quality was temporarily concealed during the relatively recent age of the modernizing nation-state." Supranational organizations, whether institutionalized religions or commercial companies or transregional migrant communities and artisans' circuits, preceded the emergence of the territorialized nation-state.[18] Social movements, such as the labour and women's movements at the end of the nineteenth century or environmentalism at the end of the twentieth, transcend state borders in order better to achieve change within them. Emphasis on the trans*regional* also accommodates the manifold subnational identifications.

Some scholars connect transnational and transcultural exchanges to the recent increased volume and speed of telecommunication. Time-delayed connections have become real-time exchanges. Electronically transmitted words may be accompanied by photos; festive occasions may be acted out in virtual presence through video connections (skyping); low-cost air travel permits families to bridge distance easily. Middle-class migrants *from* and kin *in* India participate in family celebrations – weddings, births, funerals – regardless of the continent, provided travel or technological cost is within the family's means. For low-income migrants, such as most West Africans in France, travel connections to the societies of origin are less intense. However, in the nineteenth century migrant men and women found marriage partners through correspondence, often accompanied by pictures. The delayed-time correspondence did not impede family connectivity. Transcultural lives are part of migration history.

Transnational spaces raise the issue of belonging. Are transmigrants rootless or in limbo, to recapitulate the 1950s terminologies? Recognition that identities (plural!) are developed in relationships and that activation of aspects of personality, value systems, and group cultures depends on context has made unequivocally clear that multiple belongings coexist – in fact are a requirement for the development and usage of social capital. Identities are not absolute and inflexible, they are actuated and assume validity in specific contexts. The nation-states' imposed dichotomy between members of the nation and Others is being resolved in theory and, in a number of states, in practice by connecting citizenship with human rights – from their inception intended to be global and not dependent on colour of skin. However, other states, pursuing neo-liberal economic credos, fabricate rights-deprived labour forces of segregated, often colour-coded peoples, whether they be Mexicans in the US or Bangladeshis in the Persian Gulf states (chapter 6).

The systems approach to particular societies and states, as well as to their interconnectedness through transborder migration, capital flows, commercial exchange, ideas and values, is, thus, expanded by the "trans-spatialization" of transcultural approaches: not only transoceanic and trans-continental, but transnational, as well as transregional and translocal or "glocal" spaces. Borders – separating, porous, permeable – are one aspect of such transcultural spaces.

Bibliography

No comprehensive theoretical compilations or monographs reflect the development of scholarship in migration history and migration studies. Systems theory has been developed in several fields, usually with transdisciplinary intent. All variants agree that holistic approaches capture social developments better than specialized in-depth studies.

Brettell, Caroline B., and James F. Hollifield, eds, *Migration Theory: Talking across Disciplines* (New York, 2000).
Cohen, Robin, *Global Diasporas: An Introduction* (London, 1997).
Faist, Thomas, *The Volume and Dynamics of International Migration and Transnational Social Spaces* (Oxford, 2000).
Harzig, Christiane, and Danielle Juteau, with Irina Schmitt, eds, *The Social Construction of Diversity: Recasting the Master Narrative of Industrial Nations* (New York, 2003).
Hoerder, Dirk, "Changing Paradigms in Migration History: From 'To America' to World-Wide Systems," *Canadian Review of American Studies* 24.2 (1994), 105–26.
Isajiw, Wsevolod W., *Understanding Diversity: Ethnicity and Race in the Canadian Context* (Toronto, 1999).
Mahler, Sarah, and Patricia Pessar, "Gendered Geographies of Power: Analyzing Gender across Transnational Spaces," *Identities* 7 (2001), 441–59.
Morawska, Ewa, and Michael Bommes, eds, *International Migration Research: Constructions, Omissions, and Promises of Interdisciplinarity* (Aldershot, 2005).

The *International Migration Review* (since 1966) provides the best discussion of theoretical reflections and empirical studies. In the last two decades journals dealing with race, ethnicity, and acculturation have become numerous and appear in many countries.

5
Migrant Practices as a Challenge to Scholarship

The issues that matter most in the lives of mobile people are, at any given point in time, not always the ones at the center of scholarly work on migration. All fields of research have a tendency to generate their own dynamics and often – with anthropology and some geography and sociology projects as exceptions – to generate them in relative isolation from the people being studied. As chapter 3 showed, scholars focused on immigration to particular nations or, more rarely, on emigration from particular nations, while migrants and their families built and maintained ties of mutual economic support and emotional connections across the boundaries drawn and regulated by particular nations or empires. Scholars tended to see migrants as problems, but, understandably, migrants have not typically shared this view.

In the 1990s, theorizers of globalization and transnational-ism (see chapters 3.8 and 4.5) initially celebrated the weak-ening power of nation-states, while men and women eager to move, sometimes over relatively short distances, to take a job, or to join friends or relatives, found themselves frustrated by escalating bureaucratic, legal, and even physical barriers imposed by nation-states fearful of the impact of increasing numbers of foreigners on their territories. When they did move, many of these men and women became "illegal" as well as unwanted migrants or workers, living in fear of being discovered. The power of the nation-state continues to seem very real to migrants. At almost the same time as scholars, especially in the United States, fixed increasing attention on the salience of race in migrants' experiences and, as celebrations of *diversity* became common in many-cultured societies – especially in Australia, Canada, the US, and parts of Europe, mobile men and women paid less attention to race and married outside their racial and cultural groups, blending cultures of old homes and new, and producing new cultural *fusions*. They created new identities and families that often defied scholarly and state-based categories of race and bordered ethnic group.

The purpose of this chapter is to examine several issues that have long been salient to migrants and that in recent years have also become increasingly important to researchers. Two phenomena that have moved to the center of inquiry are race and gender. Furthermore, regarding two others, the importance of transnational families and the role of the state, scholars are also now paying a kind of "catch-up" game as they strive to incorporate perspectives and experiences that migrants have long possessed as a consequence of their experiences during their mobile lives. Commitment to global analysis, finally, is forcing scholars to analyze stateside regimes for controlling and directing as international or interregional in their scope, as labour markets have often been, too.

5.1   Race and Mobility

The early studies of migration in the late nineteenth century often focused on race and were influenced by racial "science" (chapter 3.1). Although much of the scholarly work on race has been done in the context of studies of North America and of the British Empire,[1] the concentration on race in relationship to human movement is not exclusively a legacy of slavery, indentured labour, or racial science – the so-called scientific racism – in English-speaking parts of the world. The study of mobility over the longer term of human history and over wider geographic scales also raises important questions about how far back in time and how broadly, around the world, we can push modern understandings of the racialization of cultural difference and of mobile people, as well as of the impact of the experience of racial discrimination on human individual and group identity.

The social and legal differentiation of people by "race," i.e. phenotypical markers such as colour of skin and assumed genetic difference, seems to be a modern phenomenon.[2] Early studies usually contrasted Greek or Chinese and other "civilized" agricultural societies having dynastic or republican state organizations with their nomadic and "barbarian" neighbours. The "scientific racist" theorists of the nineteenth century would see such a hierarchy of cultures as products of racial difference and, post-Darwin, the natural result of historical survivals of the fittest. But in the complex borderlands where groups such as the "civilized" Chinese met their "barbarian" neighbours, it was typically housing, clothing, and other markers of everyday culture or religion, and not physiognomic difference, that distinguished groups.[3] Cases of conversion, passing, and acculturation in both directions seem to have been relatively common and unproblematic in borderlands around the globe, although incidences of warfare, raiding, and violent conflict over control or use of land and resources were certainly as passionate, if perhaps more fleeting and less extensive, than their modern counterparts. Across much of the Euro-Asian landmass, the movements of peasants and herders nevertheless remained under the sharp surveillance of dynastic rulers and imperial states, especially as industrialization and trade in the nineteenth century began to draw ever-larger numbers of rural migrants towards cities that prided themselves on their high levels of civilization and that contrasted their urban lifestyles with the backward existence of peoples living on the land.

Much recent research has concentrated on how, beginning in the fifteenth century, the "white races" of Europe used racial ideas related to skin colour to establish their dominance over the Americas, Africa, and Asia. Sharp distinctions between the so-called white races and the other or "coloured" peoples of the world emerged and spread with Europe's expansion and white European scholars' consolidation of what was then scientific thinking about the origins, classification, and evaluation of human cultures. The Atlantic slave trade and the conquest of indigenous peoples in lands coveted by Europeans in the Americas and in parts of Africa and the Pacific are unimaginable without and inseparable from the flowering of theories of racial difference first postulated by French, German, and other European thinkers in the eighteenth century. Almost all the new nations emerging from dynastic states with their ethnocultural population conglomerates turned to understandings of biological race in recruiting settlers or in defining the conditions for naturalizing foreigners as citizens.[4] Such understanding also underpinned imperial labour recruitment schemes, the scramble of the European powers for territories in Africa and Asia, and the forced removal and subordination – and at times also the outright murder – of indigenous peoples in North and South America and in parts of Africa and the Pacific (see chapter 2.5). The campaign to restrict or to prevent the entrance of Chinese and other Asian workers into the labour markets of the Americas and Europe encouraged their racialization as the "yellow peril." Such fears soon also targeted the supposedly racially inferior white races of Southern and Eastern Europe who also were seeking to immigrate to North America in the late nineteenth century (see chapter 2.7).[5] The result was sharp restriction and exclusion based on racial theories in the early twentieth century. Still, understandings of race differed around the world, as the National Socialist genocide against Jews in Europe, on the one hand, and the emergence of transcultural theories of intermingling and biological amalgamation – ethnogenesis – among mobile Africans, Europeans, and Native Peoples in the Caribbean and parts of Central and South America, on the other, suggest (see chapter 2.6).

With the collapse of fascism and the dismantling of Europe's empires after World War II, critiques of scientific racism became dominant and a new scholarship argued that race distinctions had no scientific basis whatsoever.[6] The postcolonial reverse migrations to Europe, the abolition of racist immigration criteria in North America and Australia, and the end of apartheid in South Africa have made most formerly "white" societies as many-coloured as "black" or "brown" societies had become through the earlier migrations of European colonizers. "Whiteness studies" and "subaltern studies" have emerged since the 1970s.[7] "Race" has been recognized as a social construction and the simplification of many colours into a black–white dichotomy has been discarded. Contrary to contemporary clichés, "black" had never been a colour validated only negatively: "white as snow and black as ebony" (Western World) or "white as snow and black as lacquer work" (China) suggest positive attitudes.

However, in other parts of the World, among northern and southern peoples in India or between Chinese and Japanese or among the peoples of Latin America, colour-coding and racializations have also had a major impact.[8] In the former white settler nations of the British Empire, older understandings of race have often informed discussion of cultural differences and multiculturalism. Furthermore, the vestiges of racialized exclusions and fears live on in identities formed as migrants reacted to the racial discriminations they experienced on the border, in older immigration policies, and in their everyday interactions with native-born people whose fear of foreigners could be exacerbated by fears of racial mixing. This was the case especially in countries with long histories of prohibiting such mixture or of physically segregating those native-born minorities, such as former slaves in the United States or Aboriginal people in Australia, as racially undesirable. Migrants are often particularly sensitive to the irrationality of racial difference – and some become particularly outspoken critics of racial practices in receiving societies – precisely because they have experienced and learned of the variety, and thus the cultural rather than scientific origins, of racial categories in their societies of origin.

5.2   Gender and Mobility

In a somewhat parallel example, awareness of contemporary gender relations among the mobile has called attention to the paucity of understanding about the representation and activities of migrant women in the past and about the way movement itself has been gendered for both men and women. In the nineteenth-century transatlantic moves, women accounted for two-fifths and, from the 1930s, for just over half of the migrants (see chapter 2.9). They often moved in their own

Gender & Migration

networks, but single men also brought over partners for marriage, sometimes through correspondence ("mail-order brides"). In the Pacific migrations, the ratio of women was especially low and depended on culture. Migrants from Japan and the Philippines formed families, sometimes by exchange of pictures ("picture brides"); those from China established predominantly male communities, since practices in the empire as well as admission laws limited the mobility of women.

Today, according to United Nations data, women are as likely to move internationally, often in search of work, as are men.[9] In the labour-importing segments of the world, women may even account for the majority of in-migrants on account of the rise of electronics and "light" manufacturing industries as well as the development of the service sector. In wealthy societies, in which resident women have achieved some degree of job parity, and in which state resources for the provision of care for the young, the old, and the ill are insufficient and are even diminishing under neo-liberal ideologies, demand for domestic "help" has not only increased rapidly but has also evolved from cleaning jobs to caregiving skills. Infants and small children are raised and the elderly cared for by in-migrating women of different cultural background.[10] Their presence in the receiving society's homes questions the concept of automatic socialization into a nation; their remittances of wages earned abroad support families remaining "at home" as well as state economies, for example in the Philippines, in Bangladesh, and in Latin American countries.

While scholars seem to agree that international migrations today are more evenly balanced between men and women, in fact, relatively little is known about gender relations among the mobile before the nineteenth century. Patrick Manning has presented a typology that asserts male predominance among cross-community migrants across time and space (see chapter 2.1) – migrations which he views as fundamental drivers of conflict, of accommodation, and thus of change in world history. His controversial pronouncement replays E. G. Ravenstein's late nineteenth-century assertion that British census enumerations revealed women to be more mobile than men, but only across short distances (chapter 3.1). For Raven-stein, too, men were the long-distance movers *par excellence*.

Apparently this is true only of international long-distance moves; within large states such as the US or Brazil women are just as likely as men to move very long distances.

It certainly makes sense for scholars to begin to explore how the typology of migrations presented in chapter 3.4 may be understood as gendered. Certainly, women and especially children face more constraints on their mobility in many societies, limiting their inclusion among free migrants. National policies towards emigrants and immigrants often reflect societal understandings of gender and may limit the rights of women to emigrate.[11] Data indicate that refugee-generating crises often result in migrations with many women and children, since warfare – and the high death rate characteristic of political violence – is almost exclusively male. In addition, in recent years – as after the devastations of Russian families in World War I and the subsequent civil war – unaccompanied children have to flee regions of crisis on their own.[12] Greater attention to the balance of men and women and of family groups and individuals in past migrations and in the organization of both migration chains and trans-national or transregional families is especially important.

In fact, many feminist scholars have called for the gendering of human movements, from the micro- through the meso- and macro-levels.[13] Scholars have long paid attention to gender dynamics in family and household and have pointed to how family decision-making and obligations can shape migration flows, making gender an important factor of selectivity in migration movements. But, beyond selectivity, gender structures migration fairly continuously. Special constraints on women in the sending society can motivate them to escape, for example, from enforced marriages. Women also often imagine destination societies as offering more options for wage-earning, marriage, or education – or they know that this is the case. Gender ratios in turn shape culture dynamics in receiving areas. When many men but few women migrate, the men look for both sex and marriage partners outside their own cultural circle, often sparking the beginnings of new, hybrid identities and the accommodation of foreign and native communities. In such situations women of either group can begin to function as cultural intermediaries, while also pursuing their own agendas for consolidating wealth or power. Many scholars also assert that male-only migrations fail to generate communities and that it is only with the arrival of women of similar backgrounds that settlement, cultural accommodation, and the formation of community institutions (even, ironically, those, such as the press, that have been run exclusively by men) begin. Similarly, the impact on the society of departure of the out-migration of large numbers of men or of women, the organization of the voyage, the salience of borders and the rules that govern who may cross them, along with the processes of economic, cultural and social accommodation, political participation, and the formation of new individual and group identities, can all be studied as potentially differing by gender.[14]

Just as those who move are often especially aware of cross-cultural variations in racial categories or the racialized etiquette of human interaction, mobile men and women become acutely aware of differences in gender ideologies and practices which influence intimate and public life – from rules for courtship and child-rearing to expectations that men or women "naturally" perform certain waged tasks most effectively and efficiently. Men and women can either hold onto the gendered ways of the society they have left or adapt to the customs of the new society, depending on which seems to offer advantages in their individual efforts to create marriages, families, educations, and careers for themselves. While many countries of destination have posited waged work as offering emancipation for mobile women, those women often instead fear that leaving home to work implies the loss of power they exercise within families as mothers and food-givers.

Whether older traditions of marriage or the newer rules of romantic love offer more security, pleasure, or power to girls and boys seeking to establish families of their own, they are almost always a generator of gendered and generational tensions within migrant families. More than sedentary persons, migrants are able to observe, experiment, reject, adopt, and combine elements of the gender ideologies and practices of more than one culture. Similarly, as scholars have discovered recently, movement across cultural boundaries calls into question the natural and purportedly biological origins of human sexual habits and even the very categories of male and female.[15] Both sharp conflict and enormous variation and creativity are apparently parts of the migration experience little studied by scholars until mobile activists in the gay, lesbian, bisexual and transgendered or "queer" communities of sending and destination societies began to call attention to them in their everyday lives.

5.3   Transnational and Translocal Families

Throughout much of the 1990s, social scientists asserted the newness of transnationalism, with historians countering with a growing chorus of protest. They pointed to similarities between today's global age and the global economy, migrations, and flows of information and commodities of the late nineteenth and early twentieth century (see chapters 3.8 and 4.5). Whether or not new forms of technology, such as cell phones, satellites, and the internet, significantly change either the communication of migrants separated from their loved ones or the identities or political loyalties of mobile people is certainly well worth exploring, as are the forms of communication (letters, newspapers, remittances) and images that linked migrants and their networks in earlier times. If nothing else, questions and debates about the meaning and intensity of transnational linkages point towards the importance of multidisciplinary dialogue between social scientists and historians.

Nowhere is this truer than in efforts to grasp the relationship between migration and the universal human commitment to forming reproductive and intimate groups through marriage and child-bearing and -rearing. Because migration is so often a highly selective process, families and households are separated by migrations, creating incentives for communication and further movement in order to perpetuate fundamental social bonds, ties of affection, and familial forms of economic exchange, solidarity, and mutual assistance. Viewed from the perspective of the mothers, fathers, sons, daughters, siblings, cousins, nieces and nephews, aunts and uncles, and grandparents or grandchildren who make up families, the emotional and social separations that accompany migration were no newer in the nineteenth century than they are in today's global age. Still, it does not make obvious sense to consider all these separations and efforts to maintain or to reproduce family ties over long distances as transnational, for they existed long before national states came to dominate human life or geographies around the world. Diasporas of merchants emanating from the city-states of classical Greece, early modern Malaysia, or eighteenth-century Genoa could flourish in large part because these were networks of kin who remained economically, socially, culturally, and emotionally bound together, often over long periods of time and vast distances. Individuals in such families lived lives that were touched by the rules, languages, and expectations of several societies, although not necessarily by the laws of dynastic or national states.

Migration can particularly affect relations between parents and children and husbands and wives. Distant fathers become strangers to children. When, as in the present, large numbers of mothers are among the migrants, the care of children left behind can rearrange kinship relations for decades. Fathers and husbands may or may not assume responsibility for the domestic and emotional "mothering" work of the departed mother.[16] Grandmothers and female kin may become the main rearers of children for their migrating daughters, sisters, and daughters-in-law. To be the child of a departed father is a very different experience, for example in today's Philippines, from being the child of a departed mother. Societies of destination also assess the value of immigrants in gendered terms that recognize the burdens of child-rearing on parents or devalue it. When US Department of Labor economists publicized their discovery that the vast majority of contemporary immigrants were women and children, labour economists began to interpret these data as evidence that US immigration was declining in "quality."[17]

In most human societies, families and households are foundational units of labour exchange, economic production, and consumption. Decisions about migration often reflect familial understandings – or conflicts – over which members of the family can most easily be detached from a family household's day-to-day life in order to seek resources, wages, or business opportunities farther afield. Sometimes it is the labour of unmarried daughters or sons that can most easily be replaced; sometimes it is the person of an adult – often a father – who can earn the most elsewhere and who thus constitutes, in economic terms, the most sensible migrant. The gendered expectations of labour and of appropriate work for males and females of differing ages have a very large influence on which persons experience separation from the family as migrants and which experience separation as the persons left behind.[18] The labour done by the departed must almost always be replaced by increased investment of time and energy by those remaining. In fact, those who leave may have to work out complex arrangements for the care of property or of older relatives and to make promises of financial support or return prior to departure. Gender and age hierarchies within families – mothers' expectations of children, fathers' desire to benefit from the wages of children, daughters' hopes of marriage portions – significantly influence the timing, selectivity, and patterns of departures: short-term or long-term, circular or permanent, long-distance or short-distance. Alternatively, the decision to travel together in family groups, while decidedly raising the costs of migration, may offer the only prospects for survival abroad, especially when farming (which typically requires the work of families rather than individuals) is the most likely source of livelihood at destination.

In both the past and the present, the economic consequences of migration for families have been widely recognized. Money and goods often travel, in a kind of reverse migration, from those who have left their homes to their kin and family members who have remained behind. Sometimes these "remittances" finance future migrations and reunification in the society of destination. Sometimes they are instead intended for investment, to guarantee the marriages of children or the reproduction of the family's future in the sending society. Investments in land, small businesses, or improved housing are common uses of cash earned abroad.[19] Remittances may also foster increased consumption, especially when the migrant returns or provides information about and access to images of commodities that can be obtained beyond a family's local community. Ideas about dress, food, and housing from the sending society can thus influence consumption in parts of the world that may be very distant.

To study families, and the separations that accompany migration, requires scholars not only to attend to economic and labour exchanges but to acknowledge the complex significance of affect, emotion, and sexuality for the mobile. Longing for an old home or choosing to invest emotionally in the creation of a new home is the foundation for both creating diasporic identities and reproducing transnational or translocal networks through families over time and over generations. Expressing or seeking love as a strategy for migration may change as options for communication between those separated change from messages delivered personally by returning migrants to letters, telephone calls, and email.[20] The phenomenon of homesickness as an influence on decisions about mobility, the remitting of cash, or the financing of further journeys is still poorly understood. Yearning for a marriage partner, lover, departed mother or father or child seriously influences how migrants pursue their lives while abroad and how the more sedentary pursue their lives in the sending society. Emotion influences the emergence of national and political loyalties to either the sending or the destination societies in ways that become particularly clear during periods of warfare, when male migrants, in particular, must prove their loyalty by risking their lives as soldiers. Needless to say, the governments of populations with many emigrants or immigrants appeal for support at such times with metaphors of defending family well-being and "honour." The entanglement of emotions and nation-building, and migrants' strategic decisions about their own national identities and citizenship changes, surely deserve more attention from scholars than they have received.[21]

5.4   Bringing the State Back In

Such connections between the personal and the political suggest that migrants may at times have a greater awareness – and also a greater fear – of governments, or attribute to them more influence, than have scholars of international migration. Migration studies emerged as a scholarly field from the analysis of the migrants, not of the governmental policies that sought to classify, regulate, and influence mobile people. Yet, worldwide, governments confronted with the ubiquity of human mobility have had to develop policies, and scholars have been apt to adopt the perspective of national states (and to use the considerable data they generate) in studying "immigration," "emigration," or "refugees." As scholars have sought to escape "the tyranny" of nationally bounded studies through explorations of transnational and diasporic or geography-spanning migrant networks, they have sometimes slighted the power that states have long exercised over migrations. That power is visible in the proliferation of categories for mobile people: in their efforts to manage and govern the complex phenomenon of human movement, states may differentiate between tourists, immigrants, "guest workers," international students, war brides, "illegal migrants," refugees, asylum-seekers, displaced persons, "overstayers" or "clandestines," permanent residents, sojourners, denizens, and extra-nationals, to point to just a few of the labels attached to people on the move.

The role of governments is best understood in the modern world. Yet, even well before 1700, as chapter 2 demonstrated, city-states, dynastic governments, and even classical empires developed what we would today call migration policies. They mobilized huge workforces or sought slaves on conquered territories. They funded merchants, explorers, or conquerors to spread their influence beyond the territories they ruled or to capture labour forces. They sent diplomats to secure populations and trade goods. China's great wall was built in an effort to exclude nomadic invaders. States have also often banished rebellious minorities: the origin of the Jewish diaspora with the destruction of the Second Temple provides just one example of such an exodus.

Regulating human mobility has been a particular concern of nation-states for the past 150 years.[22] Nation-states are premised on the assumption that cultural groups – nations – live most peacefully when they are self-governed and occupy their own national territories. Yet, almost everywhere in the modern world, territories are inhabited by people of more than one culture, typically in interaction with each other. When national states seek to create homogeneous populations to govern they have repeatedly mounted campaigns against ethnic, religious, or "racial" minorities and mass migrations. This phenomenon is now sometimes labelled "ethnic cleansing" – but are societies "cleaner" when groups of Others with their own valid cultural practices have been expelled? Massive "population transfers" occurred as the many-cultured Ottoman Empire disintegrated in the 1910s into the monocultural modern nation-states of Turkey and Greece and the Balkan countries. The drawing of a national boundary between Pakistan and India in 1947 provides a second example. The formation of nation-states in the Middle East and Africa and the high levels of political violence that accompany state-making have made these two regions both the pre-eminent generators and the pre-eminent sites of asylum and sanctuary for refugees in recent decades.

To a very real degree, states compete for population during periods of globalization.[23] But such desires for population can inhibit as well as encourage migration, raising rather than lowering obstacles to be faced by men and women who wish to move. Many countries in the nineteenth century – Russia, China, various German states – sought to prevent the departure of migrants by taxing them or by passing laws making migration a crime or an activity of treachery and disloyalty. At the same time, the new nation-states of the Americas encouraged immigration by allowing newly arrived foreigners to naturalize, i.e. adopt the respective state's citizenship, with relative ease. (Note that the term "to naturalize" posits that, prior to such status-acquisition, migrants are "unnatural.") Such nations also typically granted automatic citizenship to the children of foreigners born on their national territories (a principle called *ius soli*). At the same time, as rates of international migration rose in the nineteenth century, countries such as Germany, Italy, and China all changed their laws of nationality or citizenship, allowing those who left home (and often also their foreign-born descendants) to keep or reclaim their membership in the country of their birth – a stateside claim to extend its reach beyond its territory, or a trans-nationalism from above. *Ius sanguinis* (belonging through blood) allowed – or coerced – migrants to carry their original nationality with them as they travelled. Today, countries with large migrant populations, such as Italy, Mexico, and China, seek to maintain contact with "their migrants" through government-funded cultural and political programs or by allowing them to vote through absentee ballots in homeland elections.[24] Political candidates for office in the Dominican Republic regularly campaign in New York City among migrants living there. Meanwhile, nations ponder whether dual citizenship – a frequent concomitant of changing rules for nationality and movement – poses a threat or an advantage in an increasingly integrated world economy.

By the nineteenth century, countries receiving large numbers of foreigners began to question the racial, social, and cultural impact of migration and to assert that border control and even limits on human movement were fundamental dimensions of national sovereignty. Restriction and regulation of migration – prohibitions against entry of Chinese workers, anarchists, bigamists, the physically disabled – proliferated in long-time nations of immigrants, from Australia to Argentina. Governments everywhere began to demand that migrants submit to inspections of their health and histories. Nations began to require passports and visas. As restrictions peaked in the aftermath of World War I, those fleeing political, ethnic, or religious oppression found that they had ever-fewer options for asylum. After World War II, workers found they could move across borders – into West European states or the oil-rich new economies of the Persian Gulf for example – only on short-term visas that required them to leave again. Those who violated restrictive laws, whether strategically or in terror of their lives, those who failed to master the complex and increasingly bureaucratic rules for movement or violated their multiple conditions and requirements, and those who lost track of the small pile of documents required for living mobile lives discovered they had become the most hated figures in today's modern world – the "illegal immigrants," "clandestine workers," or "so-called asylum seekers."[25]

Migration has also increasingly become the focus of international relations in a world of nation-states. Throughout the nineteenth century the United States repeatedly used diplomacy to encourage the nations of the world to eliminate their laws prohibiting departures. Both the new League of Nations (in the 1920s) and the United Nations (since the late 1940s) created agencies to investigate and suggest model practices for handling complex issues such as dealing with those who became stateless through changes in national boundaries, the definition of the refugee or the asylum-seeker, and the notion of "human rights" for the mobile. Nation-states sometimes negotiate directly with another – as did the US and Mexico in the early 1940s and Italy and Belgium in the late 1940s – to recruit and "deliver" workers, sometimes in exchange for needed imports (for example coal in the case of Italy). Similarly, nations often negotiate the fine points of citizenship and naturalization rights as applied to their citizens.

In 1948, the UN Universal Declaration of Human Rights proclaimed the right of people to leave the country where they belonged and to return to it, but it created no concomitant right to enter the national territory of any other country – effectively ending the right to depart at the border fence. Entry remained an element of national sovereignty, and most nations of the world today continue to define very carefully and narrowly the conditions under which foreigners can be admitted to their territories. Especially under conditions of the present phase of economic globalization, with rapidly shifting demands for male and female labour and with the relocation of sites of production from Europe and North America to other parts of the world, the results have included huge and growing populations living in illegality and insecurity and increasingly heated debates worldwide about trafficking, exploitation, and a "clash of civilizations." Most national states continue to seek unilateral solutions to the "problem" of mobile people. Laws governing entry and the rights of foreigners are determined in national capitals, not in bilateral treaties or in UN headquarters. While the formation of the European Union provided for free movement among its member states, its counterparts in other parts of the world – notably the North American Free Trade Agreement (NAFTA) – allowed for the free movement only of commodities and capital, not of people. Mexican workers displaced from rural areas by imported corn grown in Iowa (and then re-exported to the US as tortillas to feed Mexican workers there) have access to no more than 5,000 visas a year, and as a result NAFTA's "free trade" contributed to rapid increases in illegal entry into the US in the 1990s. Many export commodities, under the slogan of "free trade" but with implied fetters on mobility, in fact displace large numbers of people in the importing societies, thus massively enlarging the reservoir of potential migrants.

Taking seriously the perspectives and lives of mobile men and women brings the salience of race and gender and the considerable power of national states clearly into focus, and scholarship has tackled each of these issues more extensively in the past two decades. While few migrants think globally when making choices about the pursuit of their own lives, the states whose power they encounter are more likely to do so. In fact it is possible to imagine a changing sequence of migration regimes shared loosely across interconnected societies or nations at various moments in time. These regimes may be only roughly perceived by the migrants themselves, but global and world histories increasingly bring them into view. Focused on the present and on the international system of sovereign nation-states that currently defend national borders through control of movement, political scientists have not always taken up the study of the migration regimes of the past.[26]

Bibliography

Frederickson, George M., *Racism: A Short History* (Princeton, NJ, 2002).

Gabaccia, Donna, Katharine Donato, Jennifer Holdaway, Martin Manalansan, and Patricia Pessar, eds, "Gender and Migration," special issue of *International Migration Review* 40.1 (2006).

Green, Nancy, and François Weil, eds, *Citizenship and Those Who Leave: The Politics of Emigration and Expatriation* (Urbana, IL, 2007).

Hirschman, Charles, Philip Kasinitz, and Josh DeWind, eds, *The Handbook of International Migration: The American Experience* (New York, 1999).

Liu, Haiming, *The Transnational History of a Chinese Family: Immigrant Letters, Family Business and Reverse Migration* (New Brunswick, NJ, 2005).

McKeown, Adam, *Melancholy Order: Asian Migration and the Globalization of Borders* (New York, 2009).

Palriwala, Rajni, and Patricia Uberoi, eds, *Marriage, Migration and Gender* (New York, 2008).

Sharpe, Pamela, ed., *Women, Gender and Labour Migration: Historical and Global Perspectives* (New York, 2001).

Torpey, John, *The Invention of the Passport: Surveillance, Citizenship and the State* (Cambridge, 2000).

Zolberg, Aristide, *Nation by Design: Immigration Policy in the Fashioning of America* (Cambridge, MA, 2006).

6
Perspectives in the Early Twenty-First Century

Migration history is becoming an interdisciplinary field – migration studies – that connects sociological and anthropological studies with research on economic conditions and political frames. Increasingly, political scientists write about citizenship or, more recently, of "belonging and embeddedness," of inclusion and exclusion, of passport and entry laws. They analyze plurality, diversity, multicultural interactions, and structures accommodating a plurality of cultures, and political philosophers begin to develop new accommodative models of inclusion and equality. Economists, on the other hand, with the imposition of neo-liberal models of markets onto whole societies, have been contributing to the mass generation of migrants through non-sustainable economic regimes – the food crisis in early 2008 being only one case in point. Those who riot because of the steep rise in food prices will (have to) consider temporary migration or permanent departure if no relief is provided by stateside and international financial institution-mandated economies that have lost connection to low-income people. In the humanities, study of the multivocality of poetry and novels, of music and other arts, has created vibrant new approaches. Research and analysis have become transdisciplinary – at a time when celebrations of diversity are being replaced or supplemented by fusion in intercultural marriages, media, or other expressions, and when – on the negative side – the recent rise of anti-foreigner violence and exclusionary practices poses problems of governance.

Along with labour mobility, refugee migrations rank high in public attention and increasingly in research. Refugee studies has become a distinct field,[1] since post-migration needs of fleeing and traumatized women, children, and men demand different responses from those to voluntary migrants, and since the legal frame of refugee admission in most countries differs from admission rules for voluntary migrants. Political and critical economists analyze the growing world-encompassing disparities between rich and developing countries, expressed also in a division of the world's people by colour of skin (chapter 6.1). Migrant-receiving societies, with their diversification of cultures, debate respect for difference as well as strategies to achieve a common frame of norms and values (chapter 6.2). Migrating men and women and their children face issues of defining themselves in relationship to others in both departure and receiving cultures. Rather than accepting being slotted into a national identity, as outdated master narratives demanded, they negotiate multiple identifications – as migrants in the past did under different political and discursive frames (chapter 6.3).

6.1 Gendered and Racialized Labour and Refugee Migrations in the Present

The vast majority of migrants do not head for wealthy countries in the North, as some extremist politicians and most media seek to suggest. Globally, we distinguish between (1) migrations within the developing or "intra-periphery" world, (2) migrations internal to the wealthy world, and (3) migrations between these macro-regions of the bifurcated yet integrated global economic system. Within the major regions of migrations (chapter 2.9) uneven economic development explains internal movements, for example from French-language northern Africa and from Southern and Southeastern Europe to Western and Northern Europe; of retired people with sufficient means to the sun-belt of the United States or to Mexico and the Caribbean; of those escaping from impoverished Zimbabwe to South Africa; or of people from rural regions in East Asia to "tiger states" such as Singapore and South Korea. The newly industrializing societies of India, China, and Brazil show high rates of internal rural–urban and inter-urban mobility. As in the past, migrants move to economies and cultures in which their specific human capital, skills or lack of them, language, and everyday practices can be negotiated into an income- or, at least, subsistence-providing position – if, initially, often only in a labour-market niche shunned by the resident population.

With the ever larger global disparities, largely as a result of global terms of trade imposed by wealthy states and financial institutions of global reach, propensity to migrate is high. According to the data in the UN *Human Development Report* – supported by World Bank statistics – the richest fifth of the world population is about sixty times better off than the poorest fifth. This gap has doubled since the 1960s and continues to grow.[2] In human terms, every day 40,000 children, women, and men die of hunger. Pets in industrialized countries are fed better than children in poor countries, $40 billion being spent on pets in the US alone. For centuries parents have opted for migration under similar circumstances.[3]

The globalization of access to labour forces and the ease of fast transport have resulted in two derived patterns of mobility: production facilities are moved from wealthy to low-wage countries (rather than, as in the past, bound workers to production facilities); and, at the two ends of this job-and-technologies transfer, individual producers or producing families have to leave de-industrializing zones or move to those of new investment. Workers deprived of their jobs locally by a capitalist entrepreneurial system operating globally often vent their grievances against in-migrants visible locally: "visibility" implies new racializations. Little multidisciplinary and comprehensive research is undertaken: political economists study the structures, sociologists and anthropologists examine the human perspectives, social workers attempt to collect data to cope with the consequences. Labour reservoirs worldwide are changing because, as in late nineteenth-century Europe, family farms across the world are no longer economically viable. This forces producers off the land, and the vast numbers of refugees also enter labour markets once they leave camps.

In the past, large segments of labour migrants targeted industrial jobs worldwide that gendered "worldviews" or social perceptions considered men's work. In the present, export of production technology, in a racialized consequence, reduces in-migration of men from "non-white" to "white" societies.[4] Work in the service sector – care for the elderly, nursing, domestic labour, child-care – cannot be exported. Since worldviews consider caregiving a woman's task, women in low-wage macro-regions of the world are now recruited for such work.[5] Women's care for young, sick, and old people in the intimate sphere of family life involves far more social interaction than that of male industrial labourers, who remained segregated on shopfloors, in labour-market segments, or in ethnocultural neighbourhoods. A gendered consequence of the export of industrial jobs may involve the creation of clerical, bookkeeping, and communication services ("call centers"), jobs which offer options to women in low-income countries and induce internal migration. Research, too, is gendered: studies of service migrations have been authored mainly by women scholars and activists, while the classic labour history approach to the "new helots" has been continued by men.[6]

Migration history, with its long-term perspective, compares the European ethnic deportations and mass generation of refugees in the first half of the twentieth century with the macro-regional refugee generation (1) during Japan's imperialist attempt to establish a Greater Asian Co-prosperity Sphere (1930s to 1945) and (2) in the decolonizing segments of the globe since the 1950s. Comprehensive migration and refugee studies attempt to provide policy-relevant data and recommendations as regards the following three major displacement processes.

First, involuntary departure because of warfare, selective stateside persecution, inter-ethnic fighting, or other forms of violence has been high in many post-colonial African societies; in Latin American societies during the period of right-wing, often military regimes; in war-torn Vietnam and the former Yugoslavia; and in regions where fundamentalist religious groups attempt to control lifeways. In many cases, imperial powers such as the United States, the Soviet Union/ Russia, and former European colonizer powers are still involved. Examples range from Cambodia and Afghanistan to Rwanda and Burundi and Iraq. Dictatorial regimes, whether in Zimbabwe, El Salvador, or Myanmar (Burma), force large numbers of people to flee to adjoining states. Such refugees do not have sufficient means to move on to the more wealthy segments of the globe.

A second flight-inducing factor has been ecological deterioration. In the past this included natural disasters such as volcano eruptions or tsunamis, but in the present it is increasingly man-made, perhaps men-made. The globally rising temperatures and the extended drought in Africa's Sahel zone provide examples. When whole regions become uninhabitable, families depart in – often sequential – moves. In the mid-1990s, when the number of environmental refugee migrants amounted to 25 million, a further 135 million people were threatened by severe desertification and 550 million were living with chronic water shortages. Rising sea levels may displace tens or hundreds of millions.

A third factor in refugee-generation involves, often unintentionally, urban development and major infrastructural projects. The building of electricity-generating and irrigation-providing water reservoirs is an oft-cited case in point. These displace local, generally poor people who do not have easy access to policy-makers to protest. Similarly, rapid urban expansion into adjoining rural regions displaces peasant families.[7]

Only "traditional" refugees, persecuted "for reasons of race, religion, nationality, membership of a particular social group or political opinion," have a right to asylum under the terms of the UN Geneva Convention of 1951 and its 1967 Protocol. Persecution because of gender was added only as late as the 1990s.[8] Based on the political theory of *sovereign* states, the Convention does not apply to internal refugees from factional or "civil" wars or dictatorial regimes. In some cases, whole state apparatuses lose the trust of the territory's people. Authors of refugee studies have criticized the "victimization" implication of the definition of who is a refugee: only victims of persecution departing reactively receive protection. People who proactively analyze deteriorating circumstances and leave on their own remain unprotected. Usually less traumatized and sometimes able to transfer assets, the pro-active refugees can reinsert themselves more easily in receiving societies. Since much of the generation of refugees occurs in Africa, Latin America, and Asia, refugee admission in European or North American societies raises the issue of skin colour. Admission policies frequently seem to be racialized, and most of today's refugees end up in camps just outside their inhospitable state of birth or "home" society: global apartheid but also racially porous borders remain central aspects of migrations and migration policies.

6.2 Inclusion Strategies: Citizenship and Belonging

As discussed above, towards the end of the nineteenth century, states with (partially) democratic structures developed a citizenship regime that relegated resident peoples of cultures other than the nation to "minority" status and forced new-coming migrants to submit to admission rules that were highly bureaucratized but still discretionary (chapters 2.8, 5.4). Citizen status, in its first revolutionary expression of the late eighteenth century – codified in France, the United States, and earlier in Switzerland – applied to people regardless of ethnic or national culture as political actors, provided they accepted the republican institutions. This has been called the first – political – generation of human rights. However, legal elaboration from the beginning or in reversals excluded women, who, it was posited, derived their status from men, whether fathers or husbands. It also excluded the property-less, said to have no stake in the polity. And it excluded all persons enslaved or whose skin was not white. By the early nineteenth century, the membership regime became culturally loaded: only those men defined as being part of a nation, the largest and/or most powerful ethnic group in a polity, would have full rights. From being an instrument of inclusion, citizenship changed to an instrument of exclusion or of the marginalization of some to lesser rights and more limited access to societal resources. From the later nineteenth century,

membership in a nation-state had to be documented by identity cards or, in case of border crossings, passports. It was
often assumed to be derived from bloodline or genetic trans-
mission and to be expressed in a national identity. Nation-
state historical narratives, the parallel to scientific racism,
opposed migrant inclusion into public memory.

The paradigm of immutable membership in nations simply
overlooks the lives of migrants – some 50 or 55 million in
the Atlantic World, where this membership regime was first
bureaucratically cemented. As one scholar put it: "That
anyone has found credible a fanciful world organized into a
collection of independent, self-enclosed political units that
exercise complete jurisdiction over a sovereign territory is
a testament to the power of state image making."[9] Only
as late as the 1980s, Benedict Anderson, Eric Hobsbawm
and Terence Ranger, and Anthony Smith, as well as many
other scholars, began to analyze this process of image-making
– once again, as has been argued in chapter 5, scholarship
had not addressed the issues lived by all those who selected
a polity other than that of their birth.[10]

Internal class stratification and the pauperizing impact of
the Great Depression (1929–39) led to a redefinition of citizenship: social rights, as the second generation of human
rights, safeguarded material security in times of crisis or of
inability to earn a living – free education during childhood,
benefits in the case of illness and of accidents for working-age
adults, pensions in old age. This again impacted on the status
of migrants: since, as newcomers, they had not contributed
to the system of social security, they could not receive benefits. In the expanding economies of the 1960s, many societies
deemed such exclusion unjust and admitted migrants – whom
they badly needed to expand their labour forces – with social
security entitlements but, under traditional views of nation-
hood, continued to exclude them from political participation.
This has been called "denizen" status.[11]

While these processes are located in the nineteenth- and
twentieth-century Atlantic World, the United Nations General
Assembly, representing the world's states, expanded the
concept of rights and dignity of human beings globally by
adopting in December 1948 the Universal Declaration of
Human Rights. With the increasing diversification of societies

through migration since the 1960s and scholarly critiques of the (European) conceptual combination of nation and state which, in its chauvinist version, had resulted in stateside violence, refugee-generation, and deportation of peoples under programs of "ethnic cleansing," a third generation of human rights came to be added: the right to cultural expression and association, whether framed by ethnoculture, region, class, gender, or race. This reintroduced the legitimacy of plurality and inclusion of migrant cultures. Two issues, loyalty and language, are still being debated, however. "Loyalty," which had included the duty to die for the nation in war or to give birth to future soldiers, came to be redefined as acceptance of a polity's structures and processes. As regards language and communication, some still advocate the monolingualism of one "national" language – a "mother tongue" spoken in a "fatherland." Such national or majority languages are, however, differentiated by region (dialects) and by different registers of vocabulary according to class and generation (sociolects), as well as by gendered ways of expressiveness. Furthermore, in most states more than one language is spoken. In India, Hindi as official language is supplemented by English and twenty-one other recognized languages. In the United Kingdom, English became the national language only after the Gaelic languages were repressed. To understand migrants' linguistic rights, recognition of the historic plurality of languages in societies is important.

At the turn to the twenty-first century, citizenship is understood to refer (1) to the relationship between individuals and the state in which they live and (2) to relations between individuals and collectives within a state. In addition, (3) the relationship to states in which migrants have lived earlier is becoming part of citizenship practices. With the recognition of the human right to specific cultural practices, plurality became the norm (or, more cautiously, the goal) and equal recognition of cultures came to parallel equal position before the law. The corollary to pluralism is individual freedom of choice: cultural groups, whether ethnic, religious, or other, which like nations have traditionally attempted to prevent both members from exiting and newcomers from entering, cannot prevent members from joining another group. A communitarian position, in contrast, would give stronger rights to communities to determine inclusion. Societies increasingly accept voluntary association with one or more cultural groups. "Diversity is our strength" has been the practice of urban societies in Southeast Asia since the fifteenth century and, in the present, characterizes the world's metropoles. As one immigrant said about his chosen society: "This country has given me the possibility to live the way I like and this is why I like this country."

Thus, citizenship refers to membership in a society with constitutionally guaranteed fundamental human rights for each and every member, regardless of gender, age, social status, position in the life-cycle, sexual preference, cultural background, or regional affiliation. People may live in their own ways as long as they do not violate the rights of any other member of the community. They need to re-examine their values as regards equal status for members within their group, and receiving societies need to re-examine implicit preference for, for example, one particular – if historically the majoritarian – faith. Choice includes the right to preservation of ways of a previous cultural embeddedness as long as it does not infringe upon the human rights of others. Achievement of equality of opportunities before the law and as regards access to societal institutions and resources is judged by equality of outcomes. The institutional frames for such equalities have been discussed by Tariq Modood and Veit Bader (chapter 4.4) and political theorists tried to frame the issues – Will Kymlicka and Charles Taylor in Canada, Rainer Bauböck in Austria, Yasemin Nuhoğlu Soysal and Saskia Sassen in the United States. Several polities, Canada being the example cited most often, grant citizenship (upon application) after a relatively short period, three to four years, as a right rather than at their discretion, provided a capability to function in the society and the will to respect its practices and values is present. As citizens, the ex-newcomers may participate and, if desirable, negotiate institutional improvements, a process which requires familiarity with the chosen society's institutions, values, and means of communication.[12]

This frame of respect for difference and of access to institutions is not unchallenged. In the states with comparatively high per capita incomes – the North Atlantic cultures, Russia, Japan, and several other Asian societies – anti-immigrant rhetoric has surfaced since the mid-1990s, and a particularly rabid anti-Muslim version has materialized since September 11, 2001.[13] Powerful anti-immigrant discourses, laws, and actual fences and walls interrupt the traditional balancing function of migration between regions with an oversupply of producers and those with demand for additional working men and women. Opinion polls indicate that opponents of immigration overestimate the numbers of newcomers present, sometimes by 100 or more percent, whether of Chinese in Moscow or of Mexicans in Arizona. This provides fertile ground for self-styled prophets of a "clash of civilizations."

6.3 Migrants' Identifications at the Beginning of the Twenty-First Century

Migrants depart from complex societies as well as intricate family relationships to chart independent life-courses in another, equally complex society that seems to provide more options. The cluster of reasons that influences departure decisions also influences the interaction of migrants with receiving societies, whether this is considered a temporary haven from where attempts are made to change an oppressive regime at home, as a long-term wage-work environment, or as a permanent place of abode for family formation or entre-preneurial opportunities. Migrants' ways of life are not deposable "cultural baggage" but are socialized into their bodies and minds. Within this frame they negotiate the new society in a secondary socialization.

From the traditional perspective of monocultural nation-states, bifurcated or hyphenated identities emerged from this interaction, Chinese-Americans or Italian-Australians, or, where more hostile societies imposed segregation, Koreans in Japan, Asians in Uganda, Turks in Germany. Social science migration history shows how cultural adaptation over years or generations changes newcomers into residents. This was the experience of Huguenots in Europe, Indians in Trinidad, and Hakka people among Han Chinese. The receiving society's mainstream also changes, whether in Malaya/Malaysia, the European Union, or Manchuria.

Migrants live, mentally, simultaneously in home and host societies, live transcultural lives. Their networks extend over continents. While the concepts of bourgeois cosmopolitanism and working-class internationalism may overemphasize class cultures, the concept of "culture shock" overemphasizes disruption, and that of a "global village" neglects cultural specifics. Problems emerge from racism and exclusion rather than from migrants' inability to cope. A 1990s Bangladeshi migrant in a racialized neighbourhood of London noted: "I can surf around the world on the Internet, I have family who phone me from America and Australia, but I am afraid to go outside my own front door."[14]

In chapter 4 we discussed "acculturation" of migrants in a people-centered perspective. From a societal-governmental perspective, this process has been called "social incorporation" in three stages: newcomers have access to social structures, they may become part of the culture and contribute to it, and they begin to identify with the new society. Flexible structures and agency form the two sides of this incorporation. "Vertical" or structural incorporation in the economic and institutional sphere include access to positions in business and government at all levels. It reflects the receiving society's openness to change. Only discriminatory societies lock newcomers (or residents) into particular social slots or strata, whether of class or caste or in a "vertical mosaic." This "vertical" incorporation is accompanied by "horizontal" acculturation in private and public everyday life. Rather than arriving with a fixed identity ("a Chinese," "an American," "a Senegalese"), people present themselves to others in particular social settings and goal-achievement strategies. They identify themselves so as to be understandable to their neighbours and they identify with the society around them according to their perceived best interests. Such identification, in both meanings of the term – self-presentation and feeling of "being in sync with" or of belonging – is dependent on circumstances. Interaction results in "embeddedness" in norms, values, and practices of one or more societies but does not imply uncritical acceptance. The "bedding" may need to be adjusted and participatory institutions may used to debate necessary changes.

Ethnocultural group formation and – initial – protection of deeply ingrained cultural practices provide a base for self-determined transition into the new society's everyday life without disruption of customary identifications. The theoretical contradiction between a corporate and a liberal construction of societies, between group and individual rights, is bridged in lived experience by societal pluralism and individual choice. Once migrants have secured their economic basis and turn to cultural reproduction, they face society-wide norms and expressions, partly institutionalized countrywide and partly specific to region, class, or gender – all of which undergo constant evolution. Culture is not static, an assumption that was the fatal flaw of nationalism; it is interactive. Identities, expressed in relationships, may assume multiple versions and redefinitions over time. Depending on who she is communicating with, an immigrant Muslim (or Christian or Buddhist) woman with one child may define herself by ethnicity, religion, motherhood, gender, single-parent role, age, breadwinner status, culture of origin, or post-migration citizenship. Different aspects assume center-stage position in different settings. This, of course, holds true for non-migrating people. But migrants, on account of their mobility between settings, are often more aware of such flexibilities.

Young people, in the educational systems of many-cultured societies, develop multi- or transcultural social capital which involves four aspects.

1   It involves recognition, acceptance, and appreciation of differences, whether grounded in race, social class, gender, religion, sexual orientation, ability/disability, or other. The patronizing "tolerance for" has become a "respect for" and changes to mutually accepted participation.

2   Beyond respect, education develops social skills that permit interaction and agency in multiple cultural contexts. This may lead to "fusion" – "*mixté*" – *métissage* – *mestizaje*.

3   It involves achieving agreement on a common frame of reference, i.e. the equality of each and every individual, regardless of origin and particular characteristics and each individual's right to material, emotional, and spiritual aid in times of need.

4   Finally, it involves developing a sense of responsibility and commitment to participate in society and share with

others one's cultural and material resources. Entitlement to self-realization is based on recognition of self-contribution to a fair societal system with equal access to resources and equal opportunity to participate in democratic change.[15] Past achievements of a group culture may deserve recognition but do not justify special status.

Life-projects of migrants and non-migrants include options and trajectories. Mobile citizens may choose multi- or trans-locality: in Lloyd L. Wong's words, "The deterritorialization of social identity challenges the nation-state's claim of making exclusive citizenship a defining focus of allegiance and fidelity, in contrast to the overlapping, permeable and multiple forms of identity." As to locations for lives and belongings, states have begun to take second place to urban spheres, to "a chain of cosmopolitan cities and an increasing proliferation of sub-national and transnational identities" (Cohen). Depending on definition since the mid-1990s or the first decade of the twenty-first century, more than half of the world's population lives in urban conglomerates. New-type polities – as proposed by Bader and Modood (chapter 4.4) – provide an institutional framework and a common set of values in which people interact. They supply relational embeddedness rather than prescriptions, and they bring effective systems of rights, options for political and civic participation, and equal and easy access to resources – education, social security, labour markets, and spiritual experience among them.[16]

Cultural identification and belonging is both an individual and a group process, taking place within a family, a social "neighbourhood" or community, a region, a state, a religion, and supra-state entities. Cultural environment defines people as Bengalis or Punjabis, Californians or Bostonians, for example. Homogenization across regional boundaries and nationality constructions turn such diverse peoples into Indians or Americans with practiced and ascribed identities and with many-layered loyalties. When identifications are developed in interaction with others, similarities may be emphasized or boundaries drawn to groups with different practices, customs, norms, and values. While the power of self-definition is part of identity-creation, the power to impose definitions on Others often serves as an instrument of discrimination. To escape such labelling, some young people at the turn to the twenty-first century choose to identify themselves as "human beings" or "citizens of the world" rather than by specific cultural practices.[17]

In contrast, concerns about the divisiveness of multicultural patterns of living may dehumanize Others or label them as alien or dangerous. Cultural differences are exploited, as in the deadly cases of the former Yugoslavia and Rwanda and Burundi, or in the discrimination against immigrant children in educational systems. Retention and change are contested ground in individual minds, in family economies, and in social groups. Clinging to a particular spiritual culture in the face of the material improvement of neighbours of different persuasion, or of images of wealthy distant societies, demands individual decisions to reject such worldly advance. Similarly, the question whether women as mothers raise children and imbue them with national virtues or have access to labour markets and hire caregivers from afar who cannot instill the parents' national culture divides traditionalists and proponents of change. "Genuine tolerance for cultural diversity can flourish without entailing disadvantages only where society and polity are democratic and egalitarian enough to enable people to resist discrimination (whether as immigrants, foreigners, women) and develop differences without jeopardizing themselves and solidarity among them."[18]

One family of overseas Chinese, which as diaspora dwellers had deterritorialized and left nation and state constructs behind, owned a business in Penang, Malaysia, and migrated to Auckland, New Zealand. They reduced their material assets in Kuala Lumpur, Malaysia, to invest in university education for their children, whose resulting human capital was to open the way to other economies and social spaces. They acquired New Zealand but kept Malaysian citizenship: "Why should a person who can walk on either of two roads cut himself off from one?"[19]

Bibliography

Bauböck, Rainer, Bernhard Perchinig, and Wiebke Sievers, *Citizenship Policies in the New Europe* (Amsterdam, 2007).

Burnet, Jean, Danielle Juteau, Enoch Padolsky, Anthony Rasporich, and Antoine Sirois, eds, *Migration and the Transformation of Cultures* (Toronto, 1992).

Held, David, *Democracy and the Global Order: From the Modern State to Cosmopolitan Governance* (Stanford, CA, 1995).

Isajiw, Wsevolod W., *Understanding Diversity: Ethnicity and Race in the Canadian Context* (Toronto, 1999) [the findings of this sociological study are applicable to other societies].

Manning, M. Lee, and Leroy G. Baruth, *Multicultural Education of Children and Adolescents* (1991; 3rd edn, Boston, 2000).

Naerssen, Ton van, Ernst Spaan, and Annelies Zoomers, eds, *Global Migration and Development* (London, 2007).

UNFPA, *State of World Population 2006, A Passage to Hope: Women and International Migration*, http://www.unfpa.org/swp/2006/english/introduction.html

The Centre for Refugee Studies, York University, Toronto, provides the best collection of links worldwide: http://www.yorku.ca/crs/Resources/internet_resources.htm

European Research Center on Migration and Ethnic Relations [Europe]: http://www.ercomer.org

Migration Policy Institute [United States]: http://www.migrationinformation.org/datahub/

Refugee Studies Centre, Oxford University: http://www.rsc.ox.ac.uk/

UNESCO Migration Research Institute: http://databases.unesco.org/migration/migwebintro.shtml

Notes

Chapter 2   Migration in Human History

1   This chapter is based on three surveys which provide references to studies on particular regions, periods, or types of migration: Jerry H. Bentley, *Old World Encounters: Cross-Cultural Contacts and Exchanges in Pre-Modern Times* (New York, 1993); Dirk Hoerder, *Cultures in Contact: World Migrations in the Second Millennium* (Durham, NC, 2002); Patrick Manning, *Migration in World History* (New York, 2005).

2   The best atlas to use with this text is the *Dorling Kindersley World History Atlas*, gen. ed. Jeremy Black (2001; rev. edn, London, 2005). In French, the *Atlas historique: l'histoire du monde*, ed. Georges Duby (1987; rev. edn, Paris, 1994) is equally useful. Specialized atlases include Aaron Segal, *An Atlas of International Migration* (London, 1993); Gérard Chaliand, Michel Jan, and Jean-Pierre Rageau, *Atlas historique des migrations* (Paris, 1994); and Chaliand and Rageau, *The Penguin Atlas of Diasporas* (orig. French edn, 1991; New York, 1995).

3   Some scholars argue that another, early type of *Homo sapiens* emerged in Asia.

4   Meritt Ruhlen, *The Origins of Language: Tracing the Evolution of the Mother Tongue* (New York, 1994); Steve Olson, *Mapping Human History: Genes, Race and our Common Origins* (Boston, 2002).

5   For a typology of migrations in modern times, see chapter 3.4.

6   Greg M. Dening, "The Geographical Knowledge of the Polynesians and the Nature of Inter-Island Contact," in Jack

Golson, ed., *Polynesian Navigation* (3rd edn, Wellington, NZ, 1972), 102–53.

7 The pioneer of this research, archaeologist V. Gordon Childe, migrated between Australia, Edinburgh, and Oxford. In his *Man Makes Himself* (1936) he emphasized material conditions and human agency.

8 Eurocentric scholarship has overestimated the role of Eastern Mediterranean peoples (Anatolia, the Nile Valley, Palestine, and Mesopotamia) in agriculture and underestimated that of the peoples of New Guinea.

9 In the 1920s and 1930s, the Russian botanist and evolutionary geneticist Nikolai I. Vavilov pioneered research in early agriculture across the continents.

10 Jared Diamond and other scholars argue that people who initiated the new techniques grew in number and gained a long-term competitive or power advantage over less innovative and less numerous neighbours. They emphasize the great east–west stretches of land in temperate Eurasia as an ecological benefit permitting experimentation with variations of ecologically similar crops. Diamond, *Guns, Germs, and Steel: The Fate of Human Societies* (New York, 1997).

11 Paul Johnstone, *The Sea-Craft of Prehistory* (Cambridge, MA, 1980); Richard W. Bulliet, *The Camel and the Wheel* (Cambridge, MA, 1975); Carl Sauer, *Seeds, Spades, Hearths, and Herds: The Domestication of Animals and Foodstuffs* (Cambridge, MA, 1972).

12 Tertius Chandler, *Four Thousand Years of Urban Growth: An Historical Census* (Lewiston, NY, 1987).

13 Martin Bernal, *Black Athena: The Afroasiatic Roots of Classical Civilization* (New Brunswick, NJ, 1987).

14 Later sub-Saharan African soldiers in Muslim Iberia were called "the dumb ones" because they did not speak Arabic; and, again later, the Russian language's term for foreigners in general and German migrants in particular, *nemetskii*, signifies persons who remain silent because they do not speak Russian.

15 Emil W. Haury, "Thoughts after Sixty Years as a Southwestern Archeologist," in J. Jefferson Reid and David E. Doyel, eds, *Emil W. Haury's Prehistory of the American Southwest* (Tucson, AZ, 1986), 435–63; Carlos G. Vélez-Ibáñez, *Border Visions: Mexican Cultures of the Southwest United States* (Tucson, AZ, 1996).

16 Fernand Braudel, *La Méditerranée et le monde méditerranéen à l'époque de Philippe II* (1949; 2nd rev. edn, Paris 1966), trans. Siân Reynolds as *The Mediterranean and the*

Mediterranean World in the Age of Philip II, 2 vols. (New York, 1972).

17 Kenneth R. Andrews, *Trade, Plunder and Settlement: Maritime Enterprise and the Genesis of the British Empire, 1480–1630* (Cambridge, 1984).

18 Immanuel M. Wallerstein, *The Modern World-System*, 3 vols. (New York, 1974–88); Janet L. Abu-Lughod, *Before European Hegemony: The World System A.D. 1250–1350* (New York, 1989).

19 A fifth region, Siberia, while connected to China, is better analyzed in conjunction with Russia.

20 Akira Hayami, "Rural Migration and Fertility in Tokugawa Japan," in Susan B. Hanley and Arthur P. Wolf, eds, *Family and Population in East Asian History* (Stanford, CA, 1985), 110–32; Wilhelm Abel, *Agricultural Fluctuations in Europe: From the Thirteenth to the Twentieth Centuries*, trans. Olive Ordish (London, 1980; trans. of German 3rd rev. edn, 1978).

21 José C. Curto and Renée Soulodre-LaFrance, eds, *Africa and the Americas: Interconnections during the Slave Trade* (Trenton, NJ, 2005), 13–14.

22 The best comparative study of global migrations from the mid-nineteenth to the mid-twentieth century is Adam McKeown, "Global Migration, 1846–1940," *Journal of World History* 15.2 (2004), 155–89.

23 Walter Nugent, *Crossings: The Great Transatlantic Migrations, 1870–1914* (Bloomington, IN, 1992).

24 France's revolutionary Assembly had abolished slavery in 1794, but the imperialist-minded Napoleon, with relations to the Creole planter classes, reinstituted it in 1802.

25 Hugh Tinker, *A New System of Slavery: The Export of Indian Labour Overseas 1830–1920* (London, 1974); David Northrup, *Indentured Labor in the Age of Imperialism, 1834–1922* (Cambridge, 1995); Piet C. Emmer, ed., *Colonialism and Migration: Indentured Labour before and after Slavery* (Dordrecht, 1986).

26 European Russia, in the nineteenth century, included the Polish, Baltic, and Ukrainian peoples, as well as the non-territorial Jewish population confined to the so-called Pale of Settlement.

27 This system's first phase was the above-mentioned Spanish and Chinese Acapulco–Manila connection from the 1560s on.

28 At this time, white-ruled South Africa introduced forced labour migration and rigorous apartheid on the black African population, who only defeated this system in the 1980s.

29   Anthony H. Richmond, *Global Apartheid: Refugees, Racism, and the New World Order* (Toronto, 1994).

30   Benedict Anderson, *Imagined Communities: Reflections on the Origin and Spread of Nationalism* (1983; 3rd rev. edn, London, 1986); Eric J. Hobsbawm and Terence Ranger, eds, *The Invention of Tradition* (Cambridge, 1983); Dirk Hoerder, with Christiane Harzig and Adrian Shubert, eds, *The Historical Practice of Diversity: Transcultural Interactions from the Early Modern Mediterranean to the Postcolonial World* (New York, 2003); Christiane Harzig and Danielle Juteau, with Irina Schmitt, eds, *The Social Construction of Diversity: Recasting the Master Narrative of Industrial Nations* (New York, 2003).

Chapter 3   Theories of Migration and Cultural Interaction

1   Sylvia Hahn, *Migration, Arbeit und Geschlecht: Mitteleuropa in vergleichender Perspektive, 17.–19. Jahrhundert* (Göttingen, 2007), chap. 1; Leopold Caro, *Auswanderung und Auswanderungspolitik in Österreich* (Berlin, 1909).

2   Ernest G. Ravenstein, "The Laws of Migration," *Journal of the Statistical Society of London* 48.2 (1885), 167–235, and addendum, 52.2 (1889), 241–305. In many countries no census data on internal mobility are available; thus scholars reduced their analyses to interstate migrations.

3   [Jane Addams et al.], *Hull-House Maps and Papers ["Chicago Survey"]: A Presentation of Nationalities and Wages in a Congested District of Chicago, together with Comments and Essays on Problems Growing out of the Social Conditions* (New York, 1895; repr. Urbana, IL, 2007); Mary Jo Deegan, *Jane Addams and the Men of the Chicago School, 1892–1918* (New Brunswick, NJ, 1988).

4   Robert E. Park, Herbert A. Miller, and Kenneth Thompson, *Old World Traits Transplanted: The Early Sociology of Culture* (New York, 1921); Park, "Human Migration and the Marginal Man," *American Journal of Sociology* 33 (1928), 881–93. Some scholars have argued for a reintroduction of the concept of assimilation. Ewa Morawska, "In Defense of the Assimilation Model," *Journal of American Ethnic History* 13 (1994), 76–87; Russell A. Kazal, "Revisiting Assimilation: The Rise, Fall, and Reappraisal of a Concept in American Ethnic History," *American Historical Review* 100 (1995), 437–71.

5 Georg Simmel, "Exkurs über den Fremden," in Simmel, *Soziologie: Untersuchungen über die Formen der Vergesellschaftung* (Berlin, 1908), 509–12, trans. Kurt Wolff as "The Stranger" in *The Sociology of Georg Simmel* (New York, 1950), 402–8.

6 Approaching issues of slave migrations and persistent racism, Gunnar Myrdal (with Richard Sterner and Arnold Rose) published *An American Dilemma: The Negro Problem and Modern Democracy* (New York, 1944). Alva Myrdal, a social scientist, edited a magazine on refugee issues, 1945–7.

7 Dirk Hoerder, "Ethnic Studies in Canada from the 1880s to 1962: A Historiographical Perspective and Critique," *Canadian Ethnic Studies* 26.1 (1994), 1–18; J. S. Woodsworth, *Strangers Within our Gates, or Coming Canadians* (1909; repr. Toronto, 1972).

8 Ingo Haar and Michael Fahlbusch, eds, *German Scholars and Ethnic Cleansing, 1920–1945* (New York, 2004).

9 Especially Krystyna Duda-Dziewierz, *Wieś małopolska a Emigracja amerykańska: Studium wsi Babica powiatu Rzeszowskiego* (The villages of Little Poland and the emigration to America: A study of Babica) (Warsaw and Poznań, 1930).

10 Imre Ferenczi, "Historical Study of Migration Statistics," *International Labour Review* 2 (1929), 356–84. For a good discussion of migration statistics in the later twentieth century, see Hania Zlotnik, "The Concept of International Migration as Reflected in Data Collection Systems," *International Migration Review* 21.4 (1987), 925–46 – special issue "Measuring International Migration: Theory and Practice."

11 In Latin America, Fernando Bastos de Ávila, SJ, *L'Immigration au Brésil: Contribution à une théorie générale de l'immigration* (Rio de Janeiro, 1956), did not achieve what his title promised. He promoted preference for white European immigrants in *La Immigración en America Latina* (Washington, DC, 1964), edited under the auspices of the Inter-American Economic and Social Council. In Mexico the considerable number of publications on "foreigners" and migrants from the nineteenth century on did not contain theoretical contributions. Dolores Pla, Guadelupe Zárate, Mónica Palma, Jorge Gómez, Rosario Cardiel, and Delia Salazar, *Extranjeros en México (1821–1990): Bibliografía* (Mexico City, 1994).

12 Franklin L. Ho, *Population Movement to the North Eastern Frontier in China* (Shanghai, 1931); Joshua A. Fogel, "Introduction: Itō Takeo and the Research Work of the South

Manchurian Railway Company," in *Life along the South Man-churian Railway: The Memoirs of Itō Takeo*, trans. Fogel (Armonk, NY, 1988), vii–xxxi. 1930s North American and European research interest in agricultural settlement migration (W. L. Joerg et al.) was out of step with the time. US scholars such as Owen Lattimore and C. Walter Young shared the interest in Chinese developments.

13 Oscar Handlin, *The Uprooted: The Epic Story of the Great Migrations that Made the American People* (Boston, 1951); Rudolph J. Vecoli, "The *Contadini* in Chicago: A Critique of *The Uprooted*," *Journal of American History* 51 (1964), 404–17.

14 Caroline F. Ware, *Greenwich Village, 1920–1930: A Comment on American Civilization in the Post-War Years* (1935; Berkeley, CA, 1994), quote p. 427; Ware, *The Cultural Approach to History* (New York, 1940).

15 A useful summary of this approach is George J. Borjas, "Economic Theory and International Migration," *International Migration Review* 23 (1989), 457–85.

16 Early studies of the 1950s and 1960s by scholars such as W. Arthur Lewis, Gustav Ranis, J. C. H. Fei, and Larry A. Sjaastad were refined by Michael P. Todaro in "A Model of Labor Migration and Urban Unemployment in Less Developed Countries," *American Economic Review* 59 (1969), 138–48; *Internal Migration in Developing Countries* (Geneva, 1976); and "Internal Migration in Developing Countries: A Survey," in Richard A. Easterlin, ed., *Population and Economic Change in Developing Countries* (Chicago, 1980), 361–401.

17 The best examples of the economists' achievements are Timothy J. Hatton and Jeffrey G. Williamson, *Migration and the International Labor Market 1850–1939* (London, 1994), *The Age of Mass Migration: Causes and Economic Impact* (New York, 1998), and *Global Migration and the World Economy: Two Centuries of Policy and Performance* (Cambridge, MA, 2005).

18 Israel Zangwill (1864–1926), a child of immigrants from Russia to England, was a British Zionist intellectual. *The Melting Pot: Drama in Four Acts* (New York, 1909).

19 Randolph S. Bourne, "Trans-National America," *Atlantic Monthly* 118 (1916), 86–97; Horace Kallen, "Democracy versus the Melting Pot: A Study of American Nationality," *The Nation* (February 1915).

20 Gilberto Freyre, *Casa-Grande e senzala* (1933), trans. Samuel Putnam as *The Masters and the Slaves: A Study in the Development of Brazilian Civilization* (1946; rev. edn, Berkeley, CA,

1986); Thomas E. Skidmore, *Black into White: Race and Nationality in Brazilian Thought* (1974; rev. edn, Durham, NC, 1993), 206–18, 272–5.

21   Fernando Ortiz, "Del fenómeno de la transculturación y su importancia en Cuba," *Revista Bimestre Cubana* 27 (1940), 273–8, trans. Harriet de Onís as *Cuban Counterpoint: Tobacco and Sugar* (1947; repr. Durham, NC, 1995).

22   Malinowski was a transmigrant himself: he was born in Poland at a time when it was part of the Habsburg Empire, was educated at the University of Leipzig and the London School of Economics, and taught at LSE and at Yale. Franz Boas, at Columbia University, was a German Jew who migrated to America.

23   Sylvia Van Kirk, *"Many Tender Ties"*: *Women in Fur-Trade Society in Western Canada, 1670–1870* (Winnipeg, 1980); Allen F. Isaacman, *Mozambique: The Africanization of a European Institution: The Zambezi Prazos, 1750–1902* (Madison, 1972).

24   Everett C. Hughes, "The Study of Ethnic Relations," *Dalhousie Review* 27 (1948), 477–82, and Hughes and Helen MacGill Hughes, *Where Peoples Meet: Racial and Ethnic Frontiers* (Glencoe, IL, 1952).

25   Léopold Senghor (1906–2001), born in Senegal (then l'Afrique équatoriale française) studied and taught at French universities and became the first president of independent Senegal. Aimé Césaire (1913–2008), born in Martinique, created the term as a student in 1935 in his magazine *L'Étudiant Noir*. He later became active in politics. Paulette Nardal (1896–1985) also studied in Paris, made her home a center for black authors and political radicals, and entered politics.

26   Jules-Rosette Bennetta, *Black Paris: The African Writers' Landscape* (Urbana, IL, 1998); Pascal Blanchard, Eric Deroo, and Gilles Manceron, *Le Paris noir* (Paris, 2001); Bernd-Peter Lange and Mala Pandurang, "Dialectics of Empire and Complexities of Culture: British Men in India, Indian Experiences of Britain," in Dirk Hoerder, with Christiane Harzig and Adrian Shubert, eds, *The Historical Practice of Diversity: Transcultural Interactions from the Early Modern Mediterranean to the Postcolonial World* (New York, 2003), 177–200.

27   See also chapter 4, "A Systems Approach to Migrant Trajectories."

28   An early integrative approach by a Dutch scholar is Willemina Kloosterboer, *Involuntary Labour since the Abolition of Slavery: A Survey of Compulsory Labour throughout the*

World (Leiden, 1960); David W. Galenson, *White Servitude in Colonial America: An Economic Analysis* (Cambridge, 1981).

29 The figures in Philip D. Curtin's classic *The Atlantic Slave Trade: A Census* (Madison, 1969) have been revised upward. Herbert S. Klein, *The Middle Passage: Comparative Studies in the Atlantic Slave Trade* (Princeton, NJ, 1978).

30 David B. Davis, *The Problem of Slavery in Western Culture* (Ithaca, NY, 1966); Unesco, ed., *The African Slave Trade from the Fifteenth to the Nineteenth Century* (Paris, 1979); David Eltis and James Walvin, eds, *The Abolition of the Atlantic Slave Trade* (Madison, 1981); Nathan I. Huggins, *Black Odyssey: The Ordeal of Slavery in America* (1977; London, 1979); Kátia M. de Queiros Mattoso, *To Be a Slave in Brazil, 1550–1880* (1986; 4th edn, New Brunswick, NJ, 1994). For a summary of recent research, see José C. Curto and Renée Soulodre-LaFrance, "Introduction: Interconnections between Africa and the Americas during the Era of the Slave Trade," in Curto and Soulodre-LaFrance, eds, *Africa and the Americas: Interconnections during the Slave Trade* (Trenton, NJ, 2005), 1–11; Laird W. Bergad, *The Comparative Histories of Slavery in Brazil, Cuba, and the United States* (Cambridge, 2007).

31 Patrick Manning, *Slavery and African Life: Occidental, Oriental and African Slave Trades* (Cambridge, 1990); W. Gervase Clarence-Smith, ed., *The Economics of the Indian Ocean Slave Trade in the Nineteenth Century* (London, 1989); Suzanne Miers and Igor Kopytoff, eds, *Slavery in Africa: Historical and Anthropological Perspectives* (Madison, 1977).

32 Joseph E. Harris, *Global Dimensions of the African Diaspora* (Washington, DC, 1982); Vincent Bakpetu Thompson, *The Making of the African Diaspora in the Americas 1441–1900* (Harlow, Essex, 1987); John Thornton, *Africa and Africans in the Making of the Atlantic World, 1400–1800* (2nd edn, Cambridge, 1998); Paul Gilroy, *The Black Atlantic: Modernity and Double Consciousness* (Cambridge, MA, 1993); and more recently the works by Colin A. Palmer.

33 Persia C. Campbell, *Chinese Coolie Emigration to Countries within the British Empire* (1923; repr. London, 1971); Ta Chen, *Chinese Migrations with Special Reference to Labor Conditions* (Washington, DC, 1923) and *Emigrant Communities in South China: A Study of Overseas Migration and its Influence on Standards of Living and Social Change* (Shanghai, 1939, and New York, 1940).

34 K. A. Nilakanta Sastri, *South Indian Influences in the Far East* (Bombay, 1949); Bruno Lasker, *Human Bondage in Southeast*

Asia (Chapel Hill, NC, 1950); C. Kondapi, *Indians Overseas 1838–1949* (New Delhi, 1951); Victor Purcell, *The Chinese in Southeast Asia* (Oxford, 1951); I. M. Cumpston, *Indians Overseas in British Territories, 1834–1854* (London, 1953). For China, see Ping-to Ho's important *Studies on the Population of China, 1368–1953* (Cambridge, 1959).

35 R. N. Jackson, *Immigrant Labour and the Development of Malaya, 1786–1920* ([Kuala Lumpur], 1961); K. L. Gillion, *Fiji's Indian Migrants: A History to the End of Indenture in 1920* (Melbourne, 1962); Edgar Wickberg, *The Chinese in Philippine Life: 1850–1898* (New Haven, CT, 1965); Alfonso Felix, Jr., ed., *The Chinese in the Philippines*, 2 vols. (Manila, 1966–9).

36 Hugh Tinker, *A New System of Slavery: The Export of Indian Labour Overseas 1830–1920* (London, 1974).

37 Jan C. Breman and E. Valentine Daniel, "The Making of a Coolie," *Journal of Peasant Studies* 19.3/4 (1992), 268–95, and Breman, *Taming the Coolie Beast: Plantation Society and the Colonial Order in Southeast Asia* (Delhi, 1989). David Northrup, *Indentured Labor in the Age of Imperialism, 1834–1922* (Cambridge, 1995). See also Kay Saunders, ed., *Indentured Labour in the British Empire 1834–1920* (London, 1984); Piet C. Emmer, ed., *Colonialism and Migration: Indentured Labour before and after Slavery* (Dordrecht, 1986), 237–59, and Colin Clarke, Ceri Peach, and Steven Vertovec, eds, *South Asians Overseas: Migration and Ethnicity* (Cambridge, 1990).

38 Vidiadhar S. Naipaul, *The Loss of El Dorado: A Colonial History* (London, 1969), received acclaim after its publication.

39 Walton L. Lai, *Indentured Labor, Caribbean Sugar: Chinese and Indian Migrants to the British West Indies* (Baltimore, 1993); Ronald Takaki, *Pau Hana: Plantation Life and Labor in Hawaii, 1835–1920* (Honolulu, 1983).

40 The seminal study is Eric R. Wolf, *Europe and the People without History* (Berkeley, CA, 1982).

41 Early Eurocentric research by Joseph B. Schechtman (1946), Eugene M. Kulischer (1948), and Louise W. Holborn (1975) expanded under the impact of the UN's World Refugee Year, 1959–60. Schechtman, a migrant from Odessa, turned to Asian population transfers, Jewish and Palestinian refugees, and others in *The Refugee in the World: Displacement and Integration* (New York, 1964). Chinese flight before the advancing Japanese armies did not receive scholars' attention.

A theorizing approach is Aristide Zolberg, "The Formation of New States as a Refugee-Generating Process," *Annals of the American Academy of Political and Social Science* 467 (1983), 24–38. The best survey is Michael R. Marrus, *The Unwanted: European Refugees in the Twentieth Century* (Oxford, 1985).

42 Frederick A. Norwood, *Strangers and Exiles: A History of Religious Refugees*, 2 vols. (Nashville, 1965–9); Susanne Lachenicht, ed., *Religious Refugees in Europe, Asia and North America (6th–21st century)* (Münster, 2007).

43 Two early studies are André Wurfbain, *L'Échange gréco-bulgare des minorités ethniques* (Lausanne, 1930) and Stephen P. Ladas, *The Exchange of Minorities: Bulgaria, Greece and Turkey* (New York, 1932). Paul Dumont, "L'Émigration des Musulmans de Russie vers l'Empire Ottoman," in Georges Dupeux, ed., *Les Migrations internationales de la fin du XVIIIe siècle à nos jours* (Paris, 1980), 212–18; Andrew Bell-Fialkoff, *Ethnic Cleansing* (New York, 1996); Gérard Chaliand and Yves Ternon, *Le Génocide des Arméniens* (Brussels, 1980).

44 See recently: Stephen R. MacKinnon, *Wuhan, 1938: War, Refugees, and the Making of Modern China* (Berkeley, CA, 2008).

45 Ludger Kühnhardt, *Die Flüchtlingsfrage als Weltordnungs-problem: Massenzwangswanderungen in Geschichte und Politik* (Vienna, 1984); Peter J. Opitz, *Das Weltflüchtlings-problem: Ursachen und Folgen* (Munich, 1988); Aristide Zolberg, Astrid Suhrke, and Sergio Aguayo, *Escape from Violence: Conflict and the Refugee Crisis in the Developing World* (Oxford, 1989); and Zolberg and Peter Benda, eds, *Global Migrants, Global Refugees: Problems and Solutions* (Oxford, 2000). UNHCR, *The State of the World's Refugees, 1995: In Search of Solutions* (Oxford, 1995), and other volumes.

46 Julius Isaac, *Economics of Migration* (New York, 1947); Everett S. Lee, "A Theory of Migration," *Demography* 3 (1966), 47–57; J. A. Jackson, ed., *Migration* (Cambridge, 1969); Brinley Thomas, *Migration and Economic Growth: A Study of Great Britain and the Atlantic* (Cambridge, 1973); Paul R. Shaw, *Migration Theory and Fact: A Review and Bibliography of Current Literature* (Philadelphia, 1975).

47 Among others, William H. McNeill and Ruth S. Adams, eds, *Human Migration: Patterns and Politics* (Bloomington, IN, 1978); Alan A. Brown and Egon Neuberger, *Internal Migration: A Comparative Perspective* (New York, 1977); Martin L. Kilson and Robert I. Rotberg, eds, *The African Diaspora: Interpretive Essays* (Cambridge, MA, 1976).

48   Jan Lucassen and Leo Lucassen, eds, *Migration, Migration History, History: Old Paradigms and New Perspectives* (Bern, 1997; rev. edn, 2007); Dirk Hoerder, "Changing Paradigms in Migration History: From 'To America' to World-Wide Systems," *Canadian Review of American Studies* 24.2 (1994), 105–26. From sociologists' perspectives: Douglas S. Massey, Joaquin Arango, Graeme Hugo, Ali Kouaouci, Adela Pellegrino, and J. Edward Taylor, "Theories of International Migration: Review and Appraisal," *Population and Development Review* 19 (1993), 431–66, and "An Evaluation of International Migration Theory: The North American Case," ibid. 20 (1994), 699–752. Other theorizations include J. J. Mangolam and H. K. Schwarzweller, "General Theory in the Study of Migration: Current Needs and Difficulties," *International Migration Review* 3 (1968), 3–18; A. L. Mabogunje, "A Systems Approach to a Theory of Rural–Urban Migration," *Geographical Analysis* 2.1 (1970), 1–18; John Goldlust and Anthony H. Richmond, "A Multivariate Model of Immigrant Adaptation," *International Migration Review* 8 (1974), 193–225; Robert J. Kleiner et al., "International Migration and Internal Migration: A Comprehensive Theoretical Approach," in Ira A. Glazier and Luigi de Rosa, eds, *Migration across Time and Nations: Population Mobility in Historical Contexts* (New York, 1986), 305–17.

49   Immanuel M. Wallerstein, *The Modern World-System*, 3 vols. (New York, 1974–88); André Gunder Frank, *Capitalism and Underdevelopment in Latin America* (New York, 1969); Ian Roxborough, *Theories of Underdevelopment* (London, 1979); Ronald H. Chilcote, ed., *Dependency and Marxism: Toward a Resolution of the Debate* (Boulder, CO, 1981); Fernand Braudel, *La Méditerranée et le monde méditerranéen à l'époque de Philippe II* (1949; 2nd rev. edn, Paris 1966), trans. Siân Reynolds as *The Mediterranean and the Mediterranean World in the Age of Philip II*, 2 vols. (New York, 1972); Janet L. Abu-Lughod, *Before European Hegemony: The World System A.D. 1250–1350* (New York, 1989); Saskia Sassen, *The Global City: New York, London, Tokyo* (Princeton, NJ, 1991).

50   The classic formulation is Louise A. Tilly and Joan W. Scott, *Women, Work and Family* (New York, 1978); Patricia R. Pessar, "The Role of Gender, Households, and Social Networks in the Migration Process: A Review and Appraisal," in Charles Hirschman, Philip Kasinitz, and Josh DeWind, eds, *The Handbook of International Migration: The American*

Experience (New York, 1999), 53–70. See also Tamara K. Hareven, *Family Time and Industrial Time: The Relationship between Family and Work in a New England Industrial Community* (Cambridge, 1982).

51 An example of integrating all economic factors with social and political issues is Jorge Durand and Douglas S. Massey, eds, *Crossing the Border: Research from the Mexican Migration Project* (New York, 2004).

52 Oded Stark and David E. Bloom, "The New Economics of Labor Migration," *American Economic Review* 75 (1985), 173–8; Stark, *The Migration of Labor* (Oxford, 1991); Stark, "Relative Deprivation and Migration: Theory, Evidence, and Policy Implications," in Sergio Díaz-Briquets and Sidney Weintraub, eds, *Determinants of Emigration from Mexico, Central America, and the Caribbean* (Boulder, CO, 1991), 121–44; Stark, J. Edward Taylor, and Shlomo Yitzhaki, "Remittances and Inequality," *Economic Journal* 101 (1986), 1163–78.

53 Michael J. Piore, *Birds of Passage: Migrant Labor in Industrial Societies* (New York, 1979); Walter Licht, "Labor Economics and the Labor Historian," *International Labor and Working Class History* 21 (1982): 52–62; Edna Bonacich, "A Theory of Ethnic Antagonism: The Split Labor Market," *American Sociological Review* 37 (1972), 547–59; John B. Christiansen, "The Split Labor Market Theory and Filipino Exclusion: 1927–1934," *Phylon* 40 (1979), 66–74; see also Toni Pierenkemper and Richard Tilly, *Historische Arbeitsmarktforschung: Entstehung und Probleme der Vermarktung von Arbeitskraft* (Göttingen, 1982).

54 Richard C. Edwards, Michael Reich, and David M. Gordon, eds, *Labor Market Segmentation* (Lexington, MA, 1975).

55 Herbert G. Gutman, *Work, Culture, and Society in Industrializing America* (New York, 1976); June Nash and María P. Fernández-Kelly, eds, *Women, Men and the International Division of Labor* (Albany, NY, 1983); Sun-Hee Lee, *Why People Intend to Move: Individual and Community-level Factors of Out-Migration in the Philippines* (Boulder, CO, 1985); Nigel Harris, *New Untouchables: Immigration and the New World Worker* (New York, 1995); Alan B. Simmons, ed., *International Migration, Refugee Flows and Human Rights in North America: The Impact of Free Trade and Restructuring* (New York, 1996).

56 See chapter 5.1 for research on race and racialization, whiteness studies, and subaltern studies.

57 We have repeatedly pointed above to the personal migration history of innovative scholars. They left the monocultural frame of their nation-state of origin. Bourdieu, like almost all theoreticians of "discourse theory" and post-colonial approaches (Jacques Derrida, Roland Barthes, Frantz Fanon, Stuart Hall), lived in more than one society and, often, migrated between the French or other colonizer societies and colonized societies. Others, such as Antonio Gramsci and Mikhail Bakhtin, experienced different regimes in their society of birth. Michael Foucault and Catherine Hall experienced multiple realities and dualist discourses.

58 Anthony Giddens, *Central Problems in Social Theory: Action, Structure, and Contradiction in Social Analysis* (Berkeley, CA, 1979) and *The Constitution of Society: Outline of the Theory of Structuration* (Berkeley, CA, 1984); Pierre Bourdieu and Loïc Wacquant, *An Invitation to Reflexive Sociology* (Chicago, 1992); Bourdieu, *Practical Reason: On the Theory of Action* (Stanford, CA, 1998).

59 Economist Glenn Loury introduced the concept in "A Dynamic Theory of Racial Income Differences," in Phyllis A. Wallace and Anette M. LaMond, eds, *Women, Minorities, and Employment Discrimination* (Lexington, MA, 1977). The best formulation is Pierre Bourdieu, "The Forms of Capital," in John G. Richardson, ed., *Handbook of Theory and Research for the Sociology of Education* (Westport, CT, 1986), 241–58; James S. Coleman, "Social Capital in the Creation of Human Capital," *American Journal of Sociology* 94 (1988), suppl., 95–120; Alejandro Portes, "Social Capital: Its Origins and Applications in Modern Sociology," *Annual Review of Sociology* 24 (1998), 1–14; Robert D. Putnam, "Social Capital: Measurement and Consequences," *Isuma* 2.1 (2001), 41–51.

60 Under the notion of sequential migration, with quantitative data already in the Dillingham Commission Report (1911–12), the network concept has long been in use. An explicit formulation is Douglass S. Massey and Felipe García España, "The Social Process of International Migration," *Science* 237 (1987), 733–8, and Pierre Bourdieu and Loic Wacquant, *An Invitation to Reflexive Sociology* (Chicago, 1992).

61 Henri Lefèbvre, *The Production of Space*, trans. Donald Nicolson-Smith (Oxford, 1991).

62 Robin Cohen, *Global Diasporas: An Introduction* (London, 1997); Khachig Tölölyan, "Rethinking *Diaspora(s)*: Stateless Power in the Transnational Moment," *Diaspora* 5.1 (1996), 9–36.

63   Homi K. Bhabha, a Parsi from Mumbai (India), studied both in his home city and at Oxford, and teaches in the United States: *The Location of Culture* (New York, 1994). Appadurai's trajectory led from India to the United States. See his "Global Ethnoscapes: Notes and Queries for a Transnational Anthropology," in Richard Fox, ed., *Recapturing Anthropology: Working in the Present* (Santa Fe, NM, 1991), 191–210; *Modernity at Large: Cultural Dimensions of Globalization* (Minneapolis, 1996); and "Grassroots Globalization and the Research Imagination," *Public Culture* 12.1 (2000), 1–19, quote p. 7.

64   Allen F. Roberts, "La 'Géographie processuelle': Un nouveau paradigme pour les aires culturelles," *Lendemains* 31.122/123 (2006), 41–61.

65   Nina Glick Schiller, Linda Basch, and Cristina Blanc-Szanton, eds, *Towards a Transnational Perspective on Migration: Race, Class, Ethnicity and Nationalism Reconsidered* (New York, 1992), esp. 1–24; Alejandro Portes, Luis E. Guarnizo, and Patricia Landolt, "The Study of Transnationalism: Pitfalls and Promise of an Emergent Research Field," *Ethnic and Racial Studies* 22 (1999), 217–37; Nancy Foner, "What's So New about Transnationalism? New York Immigrants Today and at the End of the Century," *Diaspora* 6.3 (1997), 354–75, quote p. 371; Kiran K. Patel, *Nach der Nationalfixiertheit: Perspektiven einer transnationalen Geschichte* (Berlin, 2004), esp. 5–7; Steven Vertovec, "Conceiving and Researching Transnationalism," *Ethnic and Racial Studies* 22.2 (1999), 447–62; Peter Kivisto, "Theorizing Transnational Immigration: A Critical Review of Current Efforts," *Ethnic and Racial Studies* 24.4 (2001), 549–77, and "Social Spaces, Transnational Immigrant Communities, and the Politics of Incorporation," *Ethnicities* [Bristol] 3.1 (2003), 5–28. The best summary is Thomas Faist, *The Volume and Dynamics of International Migration and Transnational Social Spaces* (Oxford, 2000).

66   David Thelen, "Of Audiences, Borderlands, and Comparisons: Toward the Internationalization of American History," *Journal of American History* 79 (1992), 432–62, quote p. 436.

67   Benedict Anderson, *Imagined Communities: Reflections on the Origin and Spread of Nationalism* (1983; 3rd edn, London, 1986).

68   Dirk Hoerder, "From Interest-Driven National Discourse to Transcultural Societal Studies," in Hoerder, *From the Study of Canada to Canadian Studies: To Know our Many Selves Changing across Time and Space* (Augsburg, 2005), 316–26.

Chapter 4   A Systems Approach to Migrant Trajectories

1   James H. Jackson, Jr., and Leslie Page Moch, "Migration and the Social History of Modern Europe," *Historical Methods* 22 (1989), 27–36, repr. in Dirk Hoerder and Moch, eds, *European Migrants: Global and Local Perspectives* (Boston, 1996), 52–69.

2   Jan Lucassen, *Migrant Labour in Europe, 1600–1900: The Drift to the North Sea*, trans. Donald A. Bloch (London, 1987); Leslie Page Moch, *Moving Europeans: Migration in Western Europe since 1650* (1992; 2nd edn, Bloomington, IN, 2003); Dirk Hoerder, *Cultures in Contact: World Migrations in the Second Millennium* (Durham, NC, 2002).

3   Pierre Bourdieu, *The Fields of Cultural Production* (New York, 1993); Raymond Williams, *Culture and Society, 1780–1950* (New York, 1958); Arjun Appadurai, *Modernity at Large: Cultural Dimension of Globalization* (Minneapolis, 1996).

4   Psychological approaches to migrant personalities have emphasized predispositions such as "attachment behaviour" or "thrill" to reach distant "friendly expanses." Such common-sense notions have not been tested empirically and overemphasize the psychological as much as "rational choice theory" overemphasizes rationality.

5   Wilbur Zelinsky, "The Hypothesis of the Mobility Transition," *Geographical Review* 61 (1971), 219–49; see also Ronald Skeldon, *Population Mobility in Developing Countries: A Reinterpretation* (New York, 1990), 109–12. In some societies and periods, underemployed members of rural families or people displaced from agriculture have attempted to return to agrarian life after a period in urban wage work.

6   John Torpey, *The Invention of the Passport: Surveillance, Citizenship and the State* (Cambridge, 2000); Jane Caplan and Torpey, eds, *Documenting Individual Identity: The Development of State Practices in the Modern World* (Princeton, NJ, 2001).

7   A few examples for studies of societies of origin are: June Mei, "Socioeconomic Origins of Emigration: Guangdong to California, 1850–1882," in Lucie Cheng and Edna Bonacich, eds, *Labor Migration under Capitalism: Asian Workers in the United States before World War II* (Berkeley, CA, 1984), 219–47; Robert C. Ostergren, *A Community Transplanted: The Trans-Atlantic Experience of a Swedish Immigrant Settlement in the Upper Midwest, 1835–1915* (Madison, 1988);

Dirk Hoerder et al., eds, *Roots of the Transplanted*, 2 vols. (New York, 1994).

8   Victor W. Turner, "[Christian] Pilgrimages as Social Processes," in Turner, ed., *Dramas, Fields, and Metaphors* (Ithaca, NY, 1974), 166–230. Dale F. Eickelman and James Piscatori, eds, *Muslim Travellers: Pilgrimage, Migration, and the Religious Imagination* (Berkeley, CA, 1990); Susan Naquin and Chün-fang Yü, eds, *Pilgrims and Sacred Sites in China* (Berkeley, CA, 1992); E. Alan Morinis, *Pilgrimage in Hindu Tradition* (Delhi, 1984).

9   Michael R. Marrus, *The Unwanted: European Refugees in the Twentieth Century* (Oxford, 1985); Mary Jo Leddy, *At the Border Called Hope: Where Refugees are Neighbours* (Toronto, 1998).

10 The best textbook is Wsevolod W. Isajiw, *Understanding Diversity: Ethnicity and Race in the Canadian Context* (Toronto, 1999). In many respects Isajiw's analysis may be applied to other societies.

11 Exceptions are infants, who arrive with their parents or by intercultural adoption.

12 For a review of the highly developed Canadian research, see Yvonne Hébert, "Identity, Diversity, and Education: A Critical Review of the Literature," *Canadian Ethnic Studies* 33.2 (2001), 155–85. For the US, see Alejandro Portes, Patricia Fernández-Kelly, and William Haller, "Segmented Assimilation on the Ground: The New Second Generation in Early Adulthood," *Ethnic and Racial Studies* 28.6 (2005), 1000–40.

13 Milton M. Gordon, *Assimilation in American Life: The Role of Race, Religion, and National Origins* (New York, 1964). Gordon, like most US authors, still assumed that one single Anglo core or majority culture existed to which immigrants would assimilate. This has been critiqued by Richard Alba and Victor Nee, *Remaking the American Mainstream: Assimilation and Contemporary Immigration* (Cambridge, MA, 2003); these authors in turn remain US-centered, neither citing a single study published outside of the US nor providing a broader comparative perspective. See also Elliott R. Barkan's thoughtful "Race, Religion, and Nationality in American Society: A Model of Ethnicity from Contact to Assimilation," *Journal of American Ethnic History* 14 (Winter 1995), 38–76.

14 Thomas F. Gossett, *Race: The History of an Idea in America* (New York, 1963); John Goldlust and Anthony H. Richmond,

"A Multivariate Model of Immigrant Adaptation," *International Migration Review* 8 (1974), 193–225; Fredrik (Frederick) Barth, ed., *Ethnic Groups and Boundaries: The Social Organization of Culture Difference* (Oslo and Boston, 1969), 9–38.

15 See, in general, David Held, *Democracy and the Global Order: From the Modern State to Cosmopolitan Governance* (Stanford, CA, 1995); for a specific, well-studied society, Yvonne M. Hébert, ed., *Citizenship in Transformation in Canada* (Toronto, 2003); Vic Satzewich and Lloyd L. Wong, eds, *Transnational Communities in Canada: Emergent Identities, Practices, and Issues* (Vancouver, 2006).

16 Veit Bader, "Democratic Institutional Pluralism and Cultural Diversity," pp. 131–67 (quotes pp. 131–2, 156), and Tariq Modood, "Multiculturalism, Secularism, and the State," pp. 168–85 (quote p. 170), in Christiane Harzig and Danielle Juteau, with Irina Schmitt, eds, *The Social Construction of Diversity: Recasting the Master Narrative of Industrial Nations* (New York, 2003). Modood, *Multiculturalism* (Cambridge, 2007), is based on the British case.

17 Walter D. Kamphoefner, Wolfgang Helbich, and Ulrike Sommer, eds, *News from the Land of Freedom: German Immigrants Write Home*, trans. Susan Carter Vogel (Ithaca, NY, 1991), "Introduction."

18 Victor Roudometof and Paul Kennedy, eds, *Communities across Borders: New Immigrants and Transnational Cultures* (London, 2002), 1–26, quote pp. 2–3.

Chapter 5   Migrant Practices as a Challenge to Scholarship

1 Rick Halpern and M. J. Daunton, eds, *Empire and Others: British Encounters with Indigenous Peoples, 1600–1850* (Philadelphia, 1999).

2 Ivan Hannaford, *Race: The History of an Idea in the West* (Baltimore, 1996).

3 Leo Shin, *The Making of the Chinese State: Ethnicity and Expansion on the Ming Borderlands* (New York, 2006).

4 George Frederickson, *White Supremacy: A Comparative Study in American and South African History* (New York, 1981).

5 Erika Lee, *At America's Gates: Chinese Immigration during the Exclusion Era, 1882–1943* (Chapel Hill, NC, 2004).

6 Ruth Benedict, *Race: Science and Politics* (New York, 1959); Gunnar Myrdal, *An American Dilemma* (New York, 1944).
7 Besides the work of Frederickson, cited above, see David Roediger, *The Wages of Whiteness: Race and the Making of the American Working Class* (rev. edn, New York, 1999); Ranajit Guha, ed., *Subaltern Studies I: Writings on South Asian History and Society* (New Delhi, 1982).
8 Frank Dikotter, ed., *The Construction of Racial Identity in China and Japan: Historical and Contemporary Perspectives* (London, 1997); France W. Twine, *Racism in a Racial Democracy: The Maintenance of White Supremacy in Brazil* (New Brunswick, NJ, 1998).
9 UN Fund for Population Activities, *State of the World Population 2006: A Passage to Hope – Women and International Migration* (New York, 2006).
10 Barbara Ehrenreich and Arlie Hochschild, eds, *Global Woman: Nannies, Maids, and Sex Workers in the New Economy* (New York, 2003).
11 Nana Oishi, *Women in Motion: Globalization, State Policies, and Labor Migration in Asia* (Stanford, CA, 2005).
12 The "lost boys" of Sudan are an example from the late 1990s and early 2000s; *Aman: The Story of a Somali Girl*, as told to Virginia Lee Barnes and Janice Boddy (New York, 1994), provides a young woman's perspective.
13 Sarah Mahler and Patricia Pessar, "Gendered Geographies of Power: Analyzing Gender across Transnational Spaces," *Identities* 7 (2001), 441–59.
14 Katharine M. Donato, "Understanding U.S. Immigration: Why Some Countries Send Women and Others Send Men," in Donna Gabaccia, ed., *Seeking Common Ground: Female Immigration to the United States* (Westport, CT, 1992), 159–84; Gabaccia, "Women of the Mass Migrations: From Minority to Majority, 1820–1930," in Dirk Hoerder and Leslie Page Moch, eds, *European Migrants: Global and Local Perspectives* (Boston, 1996), 90–111.
15 Martin F. Manalansan, "Queer Intersections: Sexuality and Gender in Migration Studies," *International Migration Review* 40 (2006), 11, 224–49; Eithne Luibheid, *Entry Denied: Controlling Sexuality at the Border* (Minneapolis, 2002).
16 Pierrette Hondagneu-Sotelo and Ernestine Avila, "I'm Here but I'm There: The Meanings of Latina Transnational Motherhood," *Gender & Society* 11.5 (1997), 548–71; Rhacel Salazar Parreñas, *Children of Global Migration: Transnational Families and Gendered Woes* (Stanford, CA, 2005).

17   M. Houston et al., "Female Predominance of Immigration to the U.S.," *International Migration Review* 18.4 (1984), 908–63.

18   Linda Reeder, *Widows in White: Migration and the Transformation of Rural Italian Women* (Toronto, 2003).

19   Madeline Hsu, *Dreaming of Gold, Dreaming of Home: Transnationalism and Migration between the United States and China, 1882–1943* (Stanford, CA, 2002); J. E. Taylor, "The New Economics of Labour Migration and the Role of Remittances in the Migration Process," *International Migration* 37 (1999), 63–87.

20   Nicole Constable, *Romance on a Global Stage: Pen Pals, Virtual Ethnography, and "Mail Order" Marriages* (Berkeley, CA, 2003).

21   Loretta Baldassar and Donna R. Gabaccia, eds, *Intimacy across Borders: Making Italians in a Mobile World* (New York, 2009).

22   Andreas Fahrmeir, Olivier Faron, and Patrick Weil, *Migration Control in the North Atlantic World: The Evolution of State Practices in Europe and the United States from the French Revolution to the Inter-War Period* (Oxford, 2003).

23   David Cook-Martin, "Soldiers and Wayward Women: Gendered Citizenship, and Migration Policy in Argentina, Italy, and Spain since 1850," *Citizenship Studies* 10.5 (2006), 571–90.

24   Mark Choate, "Sending States' Transnational Interventions in Politics, Culture, and Economics: The Historical Example of Italy," *International Migration Review* 41.3 (2007), 728–68.

25   Mae M. Ngai, "The Strange Career of the Illegal Alien: Immigration Restriction and Deportation Policy in the United States, 1921–1965," *Law and History Review* 21.1 (2003), 69–107.

26   Caroline B. Brettell and James F. Hollifield, *Migration Theory: Talking across Disciplines* (New York, 1900).

Chapter 6   Perspectives in the Early Twenty-First Century

1   The best-known refugee studies centers are those of York University, Toronto, and Oxford University, Oxford.

2   United Nations Development Program, *Human Development Report* [annual] (New York and Oxford, 1990–); Dieter Nohlen and Franz Nuscheler, *Handbuch der Dritten Welt*, 8 vols. (2nd rev. edn, Hamburg, 1983); Michael P. Todaro (for

the International Labour Office), *Internal Migration in Developing Countries: A Review of Theory, Evidence, Methodology and Research Priorities* (Geneva, 1976); UN Economic and Social Commission for Asia and the Pacific, *Migration and Urbanization in Asia and the Pacific: Interrelationships with Socio-Economic Development and Evolving Policy Issues* (New York, 1992); World Bank, *World Development Report 1995: Workers in an Integrating World* (Oxford, 1995).

3   For visual representations of the inequalities, see Michael Kidron and Ronald Segal, *The State of the World Atlas* (New York, 1981), and Dan Smith, *Penguin State of the World Atlas* (1986; 7th edn, London, 2003).

4   Robin Cohen, *The New Helots: Migrants in the International Division of Labour* (Aldershot, 1987); Nigel Harris, *New Untouchables: Immigration and the New World Worker* (New York, 1995); B. Singh Bolaria and Rosemary von Elling Bolaria, eds, *International Labour Migrations* (New York, 1997); Donna Gabaccia, "Women of the Mass Migrations: From Minority to Majority, 1820–1930," in Dirk Hoerder and Leslie Page Moch, eds, *European Migrants: Global and Local Perspectives* (Boston, 1996), 90–111.

5   Another service-sector migration is that of women from low-income countries for sex work to high-income countries or in "Third World" tourist ghettos. This, often forced, migration involves high levels of human trafficking and coerced sexual labour.

6   Pierrette Hondagneu-Sotelo, "Affluent Players in the Informal Economy: Employers of Paid Domestic Workers," *International Journal of Sociology and Social Policy* 17.3–4 (1997), 130–58; Sedef Arat-Koc, "From 'Mothers of the Nation' to Migrant Workers," in Abigail B. Bakan and Daiva Stasiulis, eds, *Not One of the Family: Foreign Domestic Workers in Canada* (Toronto, 1997), 53–80; Annie Phizacklea, "Migration and Globalization: A Feminist Perspective," in Khalid Koser and Helma Lutz, eds, *The New Migration in Europe: Social Constructions and Social Realities* (London, 1998); Bridget Anderson, *Doing the Dirty Work? The Global Politics of Domestic Labour* (London, 2000); Grace Chang, *Disposable Domestics: Immigrant Women Workers in the Global Economy* (Cambridge, MA, 2000); Rhacel Salazar Parreñas, *Servants of Globalization: Women, Migration, and Domestic Work* (Stanford, CA, 2001).

7   Norman Myers and Jennifer Kent, *Environmental Exodus: An Emerging Crisis in the Global Arena* (Washington, DC, 1995);

Arthur H. Westing, "Population, Desertification, and Migration," *Environmental Conservation* 21 (1994), 110–14; Gerald O'Barney et al., *The Global 2000 Report to the President: Entering the 21st Century*, 2 vols. (Washington, DC, 1980).

8 Seminal early studies include Lucy Bonnerjea, *Shaming the World: The Needs of Women Refugees* (London, 1985), and Anders B. Johnsson, "The International Protection of Women Refugees: A Summary of Principal Problems and Issues," *International Journal of Refugee Law* 1.2 (1989), 221–31.

9 Thomas A. Aleinikoff and Douglass B. Klusmeyer, eds, *Citizenship Today: Global Perspectives and Practices* (Washington, DC, 2001), quote p. 3; Ruth Lister, *Citizenship: Feminist Perspectives* (London, 1997); John Torpey, *The Invention of the Passport: Surveillance, Citizenship and the State* (Cambridge, 2000).

10 Benedict Anderson, *Imagined Communities: Reflections on the Origin and Spread of Nationalism* (1983; 3rd edn, London, 1986); Eric J. Hobsbawm and Terence Ranger, eds, *The Invention of Tradition* (Cambridge, 1983); Anthony D. Smith, *Myths and Memories of the Nation* (Oxford, 1999); Gérard Noiriel, *Le Creuset français: Histoire de l'immigration XIXe–XXe siècles* (Paris, 1988), trans. Geoffroy de Laforcade as *The French Melting Pot: Immigration, Citizenship, and National Identity* (Minneapolis, 1996). For a trans-European perspective, see Dirk Hoerder and Inge Blank, "Ethnic and National Consciousness from the Enlightenment to the 1880s," in Hoerder et al., eds, *Roots of the Transplanted*, 2 vols. (Boulder, CO, 1994), 1.37–110.

11 T. H. Marshall, *Class, Citizenship, and Social Development* (1949; Westport, CT, 1976); Tomas Hammar, *Democracy and the Nation-State: Aliens, Denizens, and Citizens in a World of International Migration* (Aldershot, 1990).

12 Based on Yvonne M. Hébert, ed., *Citizenship in Transformation in Canada* (Toronto, 2003), and Thomas A. Aleinikoff and Douglass B. Klusmeyer, eds, *Citizenship Today: Global Perspectives and Practices* (Washington, DC, 2001). Arguments that citizenship regimes reflect a country's national character, as made by Rogers Brubaker for France and Germany, have been replaced by more emphasis on institutional practices and convergence of legal frames.

13 There is little public memory of another 9/11 terrorist attack: the 1973 bombing of Chile's presidential palace by forces of General Pinochet supported by US governmental agencies.

14 Iain Chambers, *Migrancy, Culture, Identity* (London, 1994); James Clifford, "Travelling Cultures," in Lawrence Grossberg, Cary Nelson, and Paula Treichler, eds, *Cultural Studies* (London, 1992); Stuart Hall, "Minimal Selves," in L. Appignanesi, ed., *Identity: The Real Me: Post-Modernism and the Question of Identity* (London, 1987), 44.

15 M. Lee Manning and Leroy G. Baruth, *Multicultural Education of Children and Adolescents* (1991; 3rd edn, Boston, 2000); Yvonne Hébert, "Identity, Diversity, and Education: A Critical Review of the Literature," *Canadian Ethnic Studies* 33.3 (2001), 155–85.

16 Lloyd L. Wong, "Home away from Home: Deterritorialized Identity and State Citizenship Policy," unpublished paper presented at the fifteenth biennial conference of the Canadian Studies Association, Toronto, March 2000; Aihwa Ong, "On the Edge of Empires: Flexible Citizenship among Chinese in the Diaspora," *Positions* 1.3 (1993), 745–78; Robin Cohen, *Global Diasporas* (Seattle, 1997), quote p. 175. Saskia Sassen, *Cities in a World Economy* (Thousand Oaks, CA, 2006), and Sassen, ed., *Global Networks, Linked Cities* (New York, 2002).

17 Wsevolod W. Isajiw, "Definitions and Dimensions of Ethnicity: A Theoretical Framework," in *Challenges of Measuring an Ethnic World: Science, Politics and Reality* (Ottawa, 1992), 407–27; Danielle Juteau, "The Production of Ethnicity: Material and Ideal Dimensions," unpublished paper presented at the American Sociological Association annual meeting, Cincinnati, August 1991; Dirk Hoerder, "Ethnic Cultures under Multiculturalism: Retention or Change," in Hans Braun and Wolfgang Klooss, eds, *Multiculturalism in North America and Europe: Social Practices, Literary Visions* (Trier, 1994), 82–102.

18 Verena Stolcke, "Talking Culture: New Boundaries, New Rhetorics of Exclusion in Europe," *Current Anthropology* 36 (1995), 1–24, quote p. 13.

19 Cited in Donald M. Nonini, "Shifting Identities, Positioned Imaginaries: Transnational Traversals and Reversals by Malaysian Chinese," in Aihwa Ong and Nonini, eds, *Ungrounded Empires: The Cultural Politics of Modern Chinese Transnationalism* (London, 1997), 203–27, quote p. 211.

Index

CPSIA information can be obtained at www.ICGtesting.com
Printed in the USA
LVOW10s2018220216

476256LV00009B/43/P